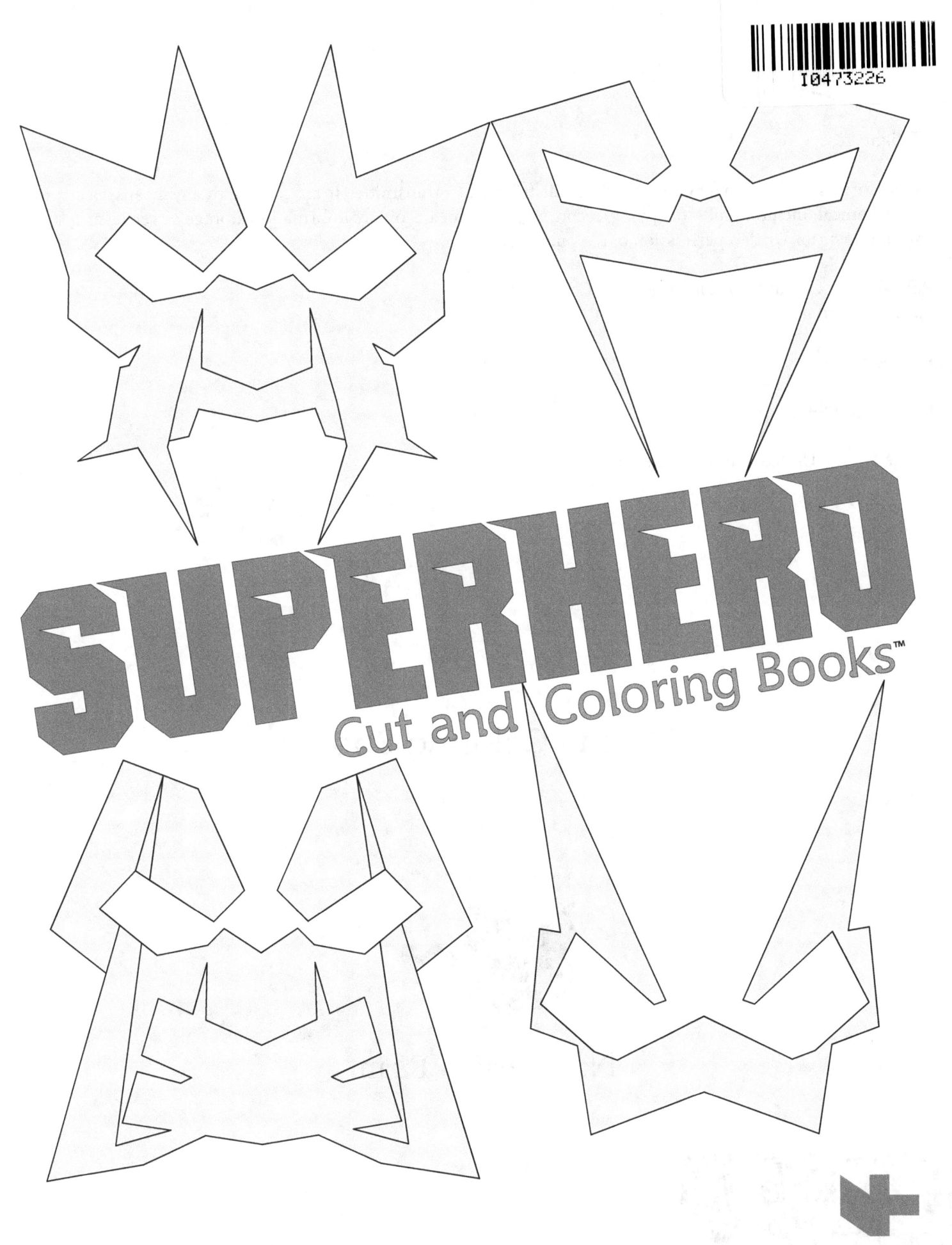

Published by Cut and Coloring Books, LLC.
Lansing, Michigan

First edition October 2018

ISBN: 978-0-9995343-1-1

Printed in the United States of America.

Cut and Coloring Books.

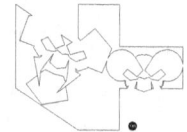

is a complete partner with

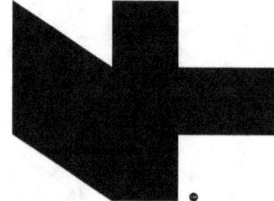

NH Design Firm.

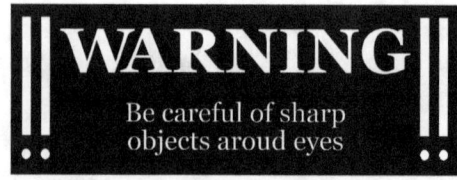

WARNING
Be careful of sharp
objects aroud eyes

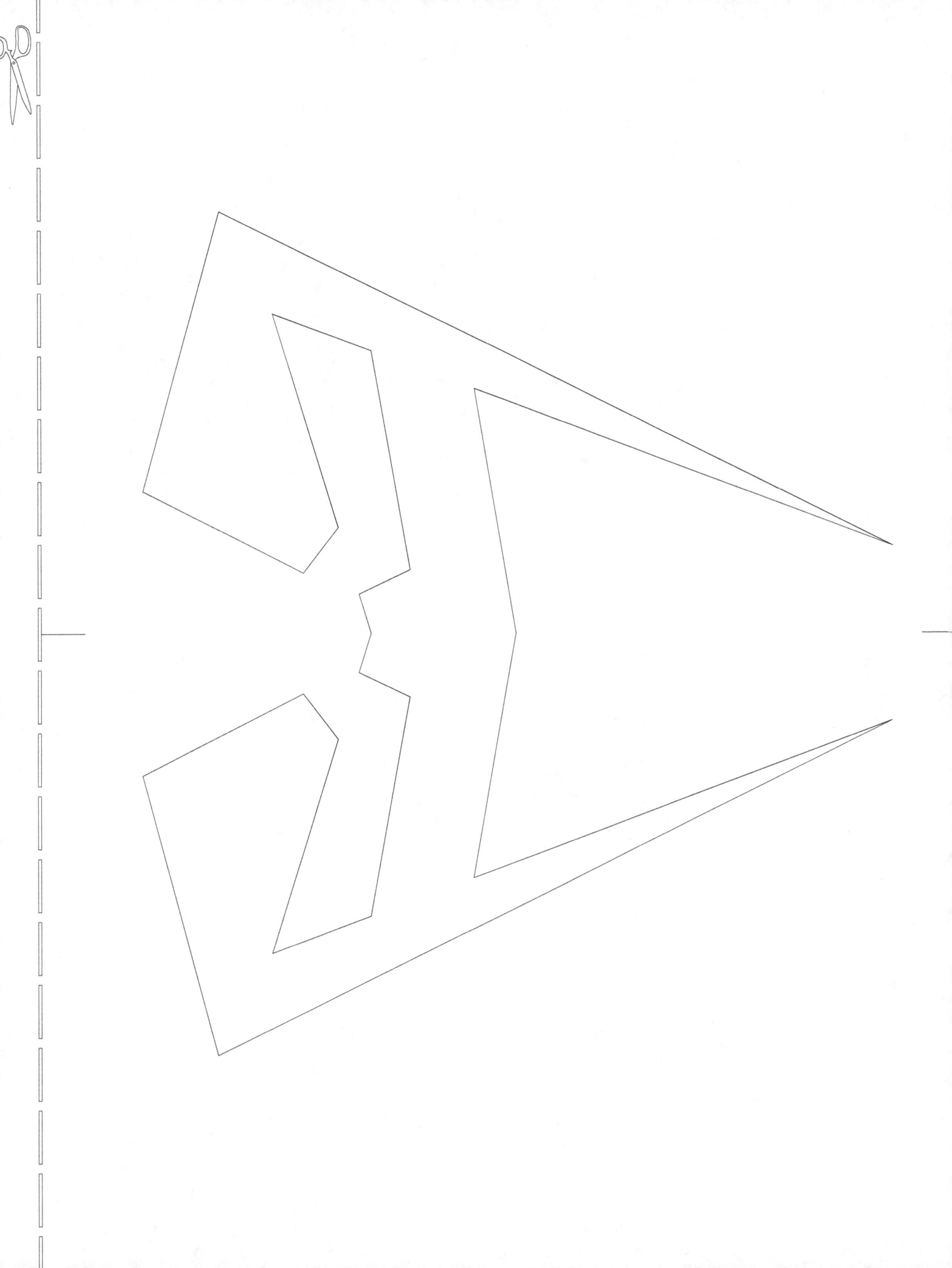

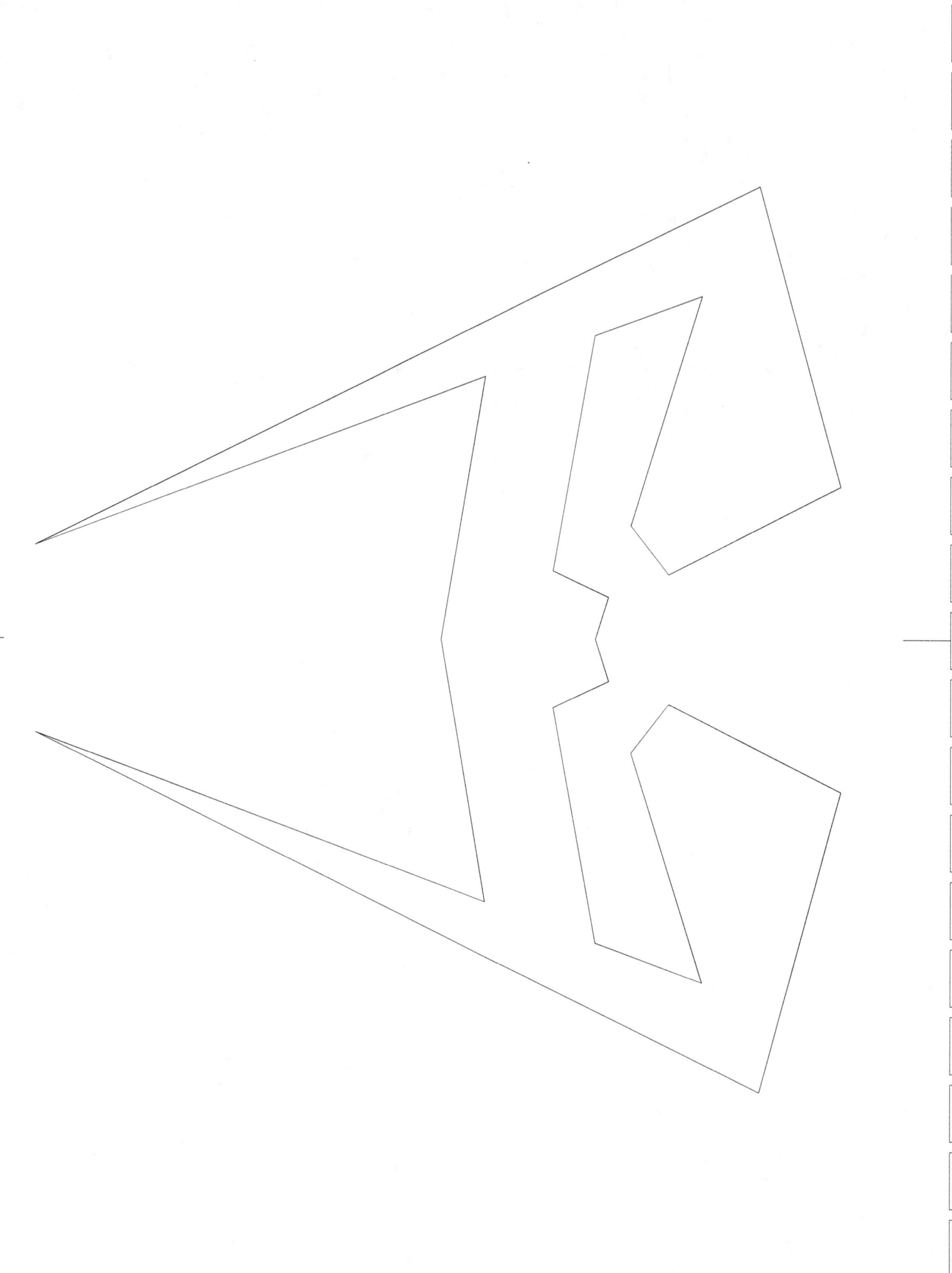

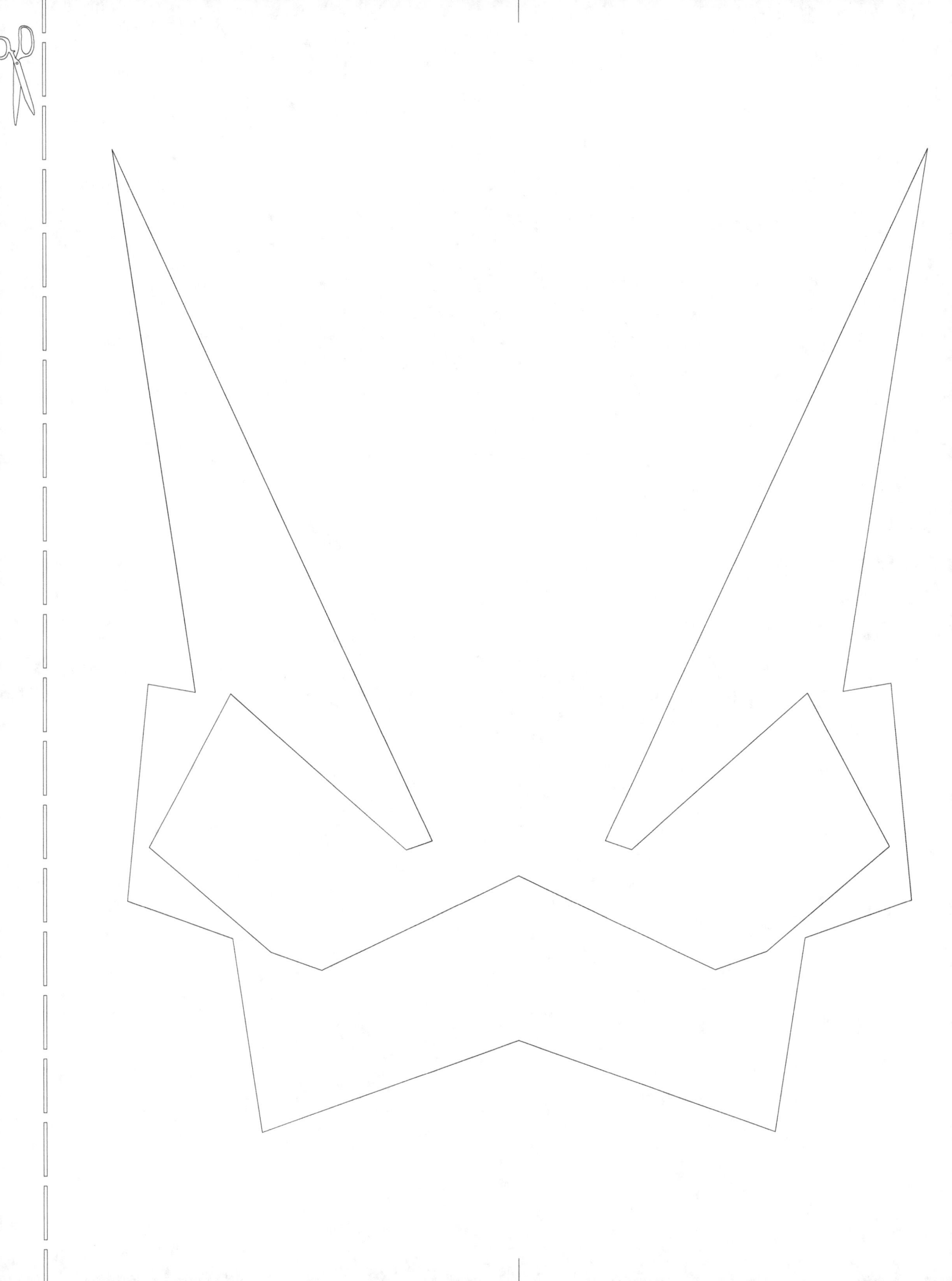

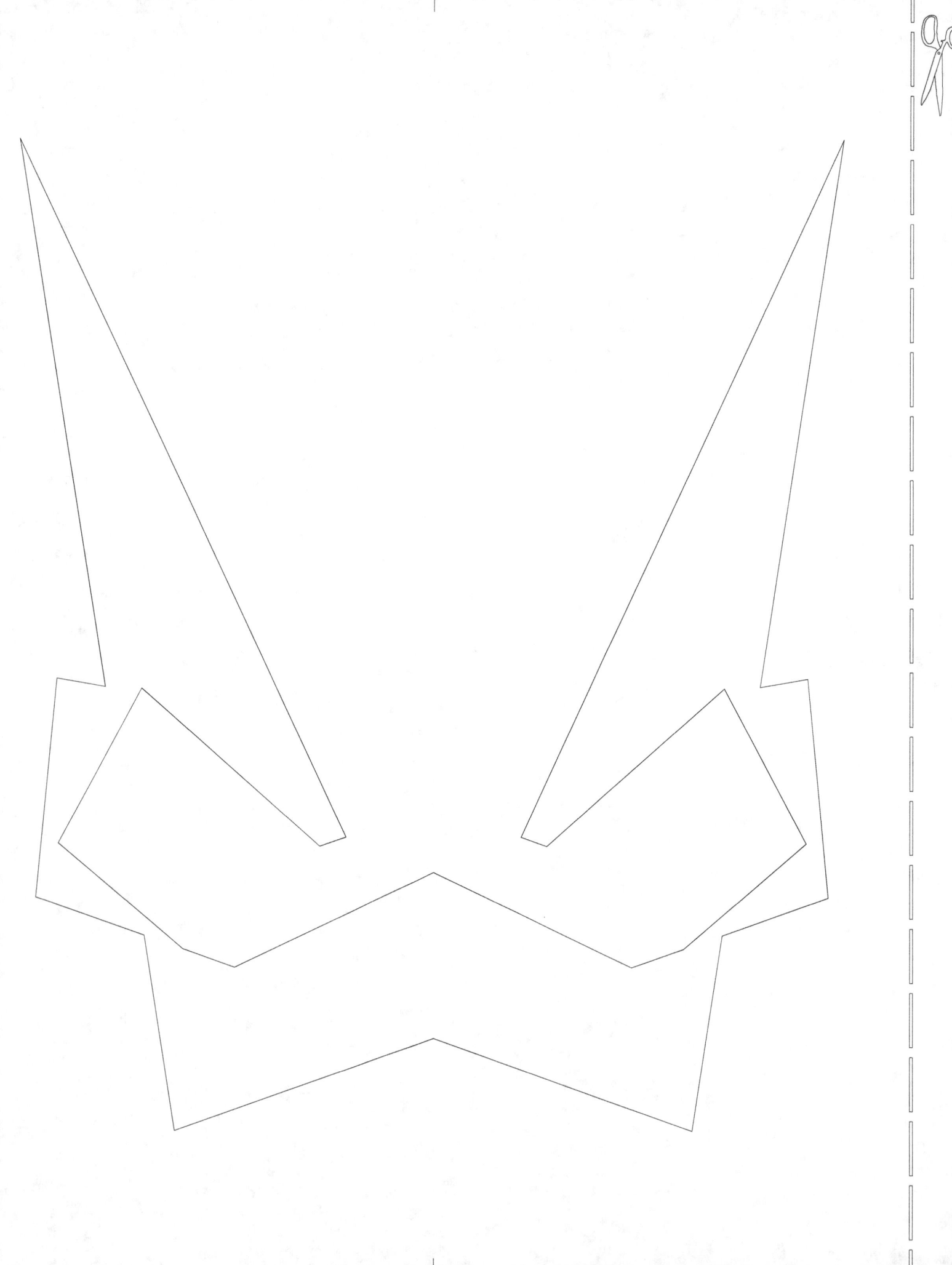

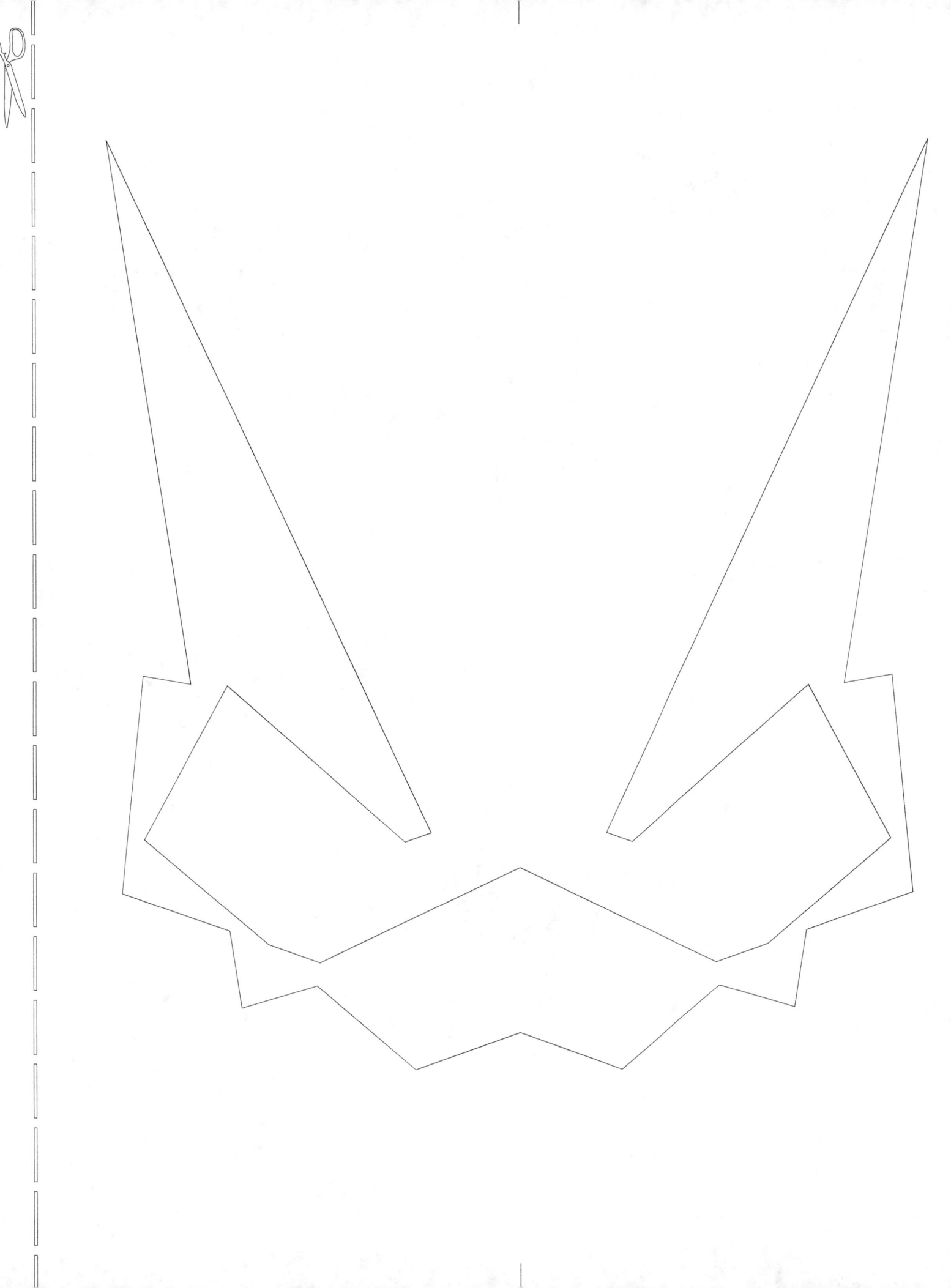

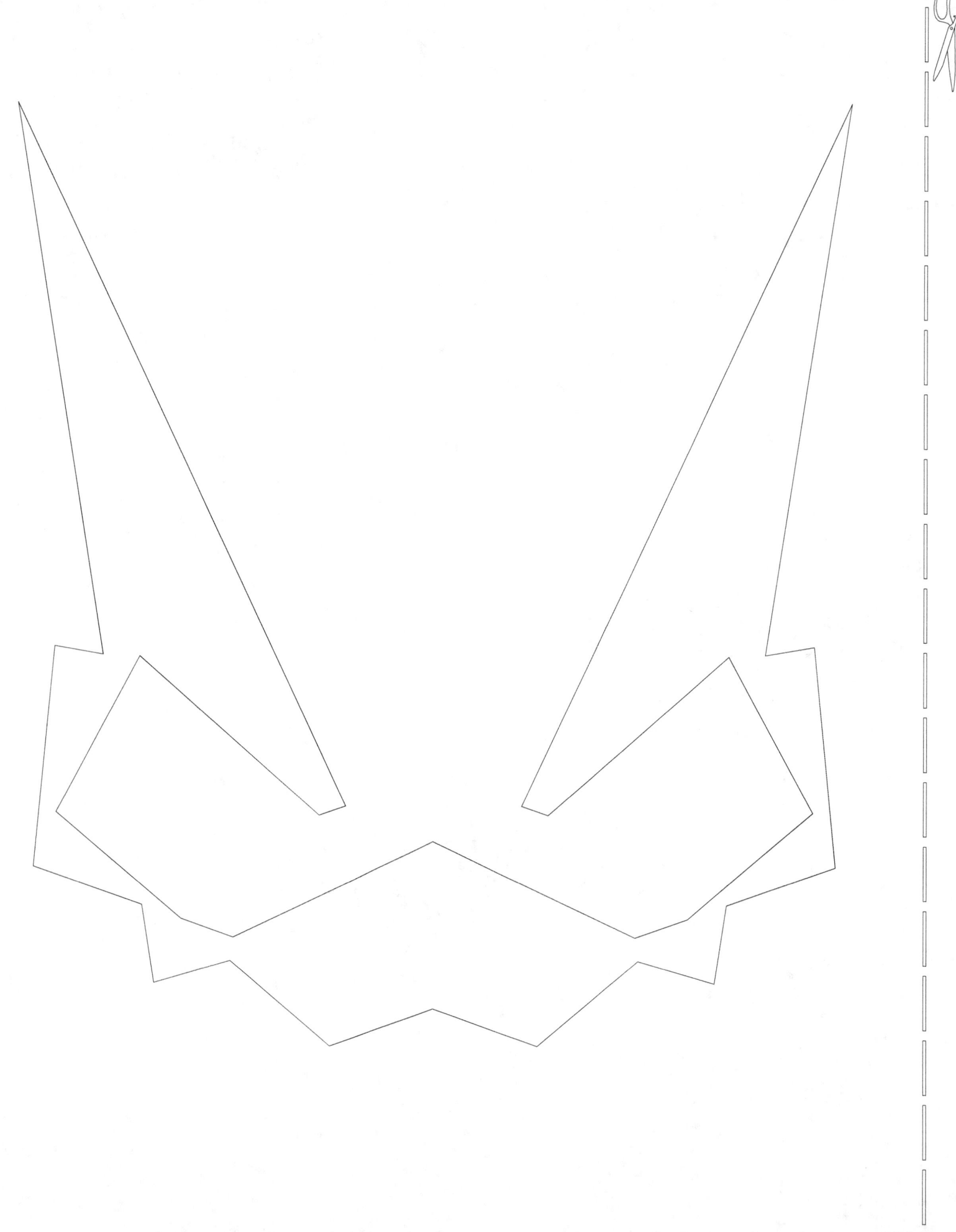

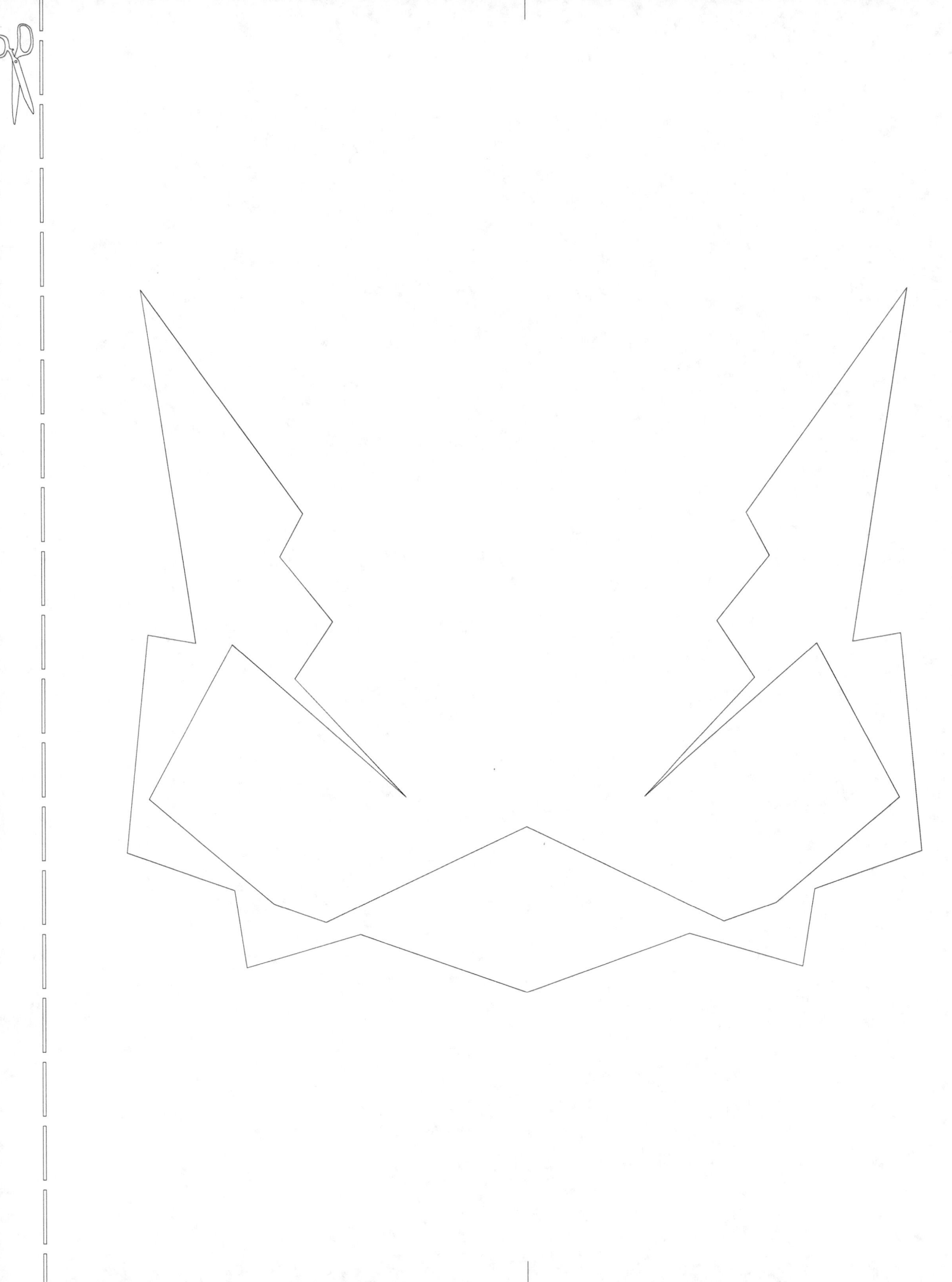

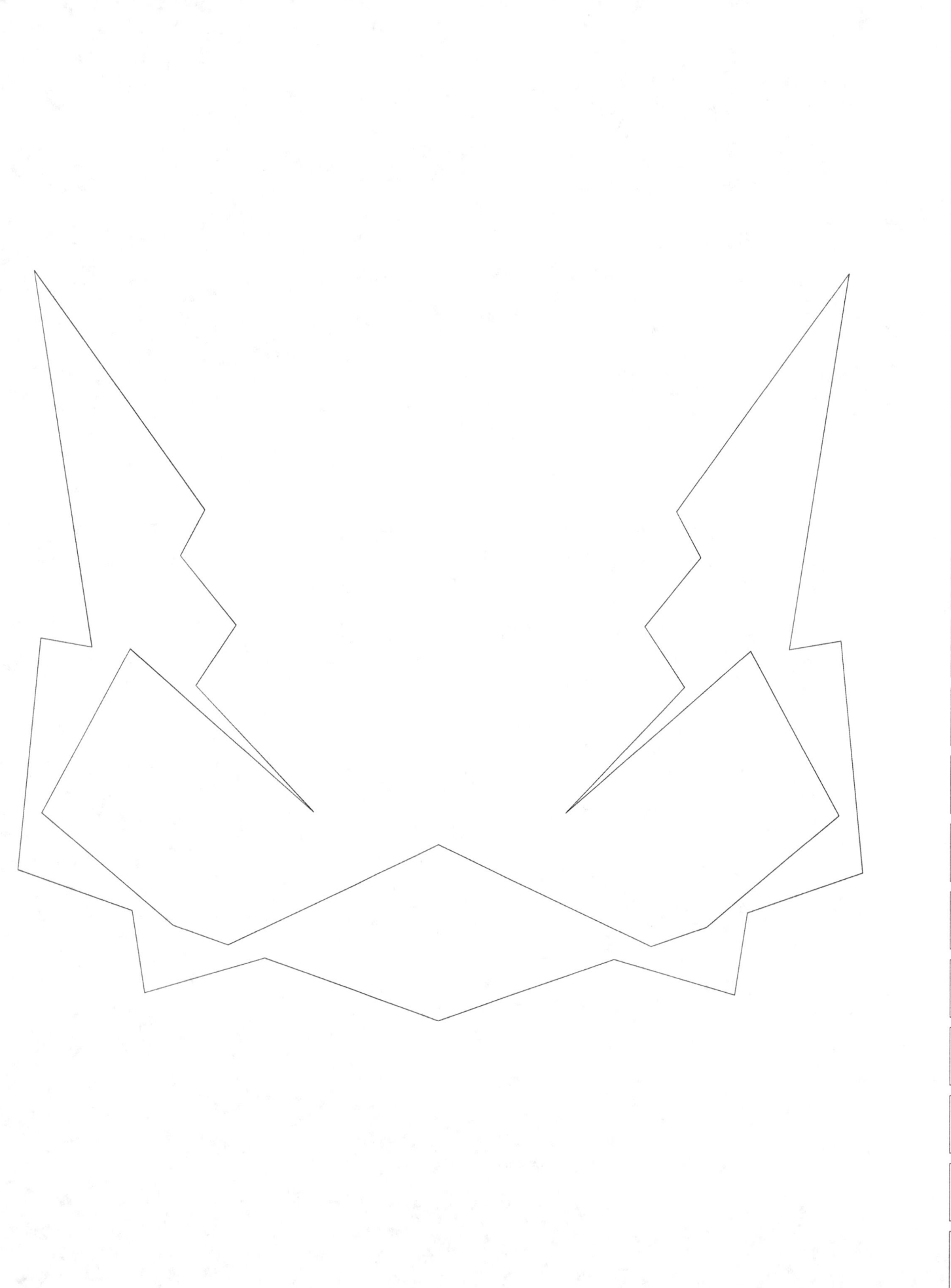

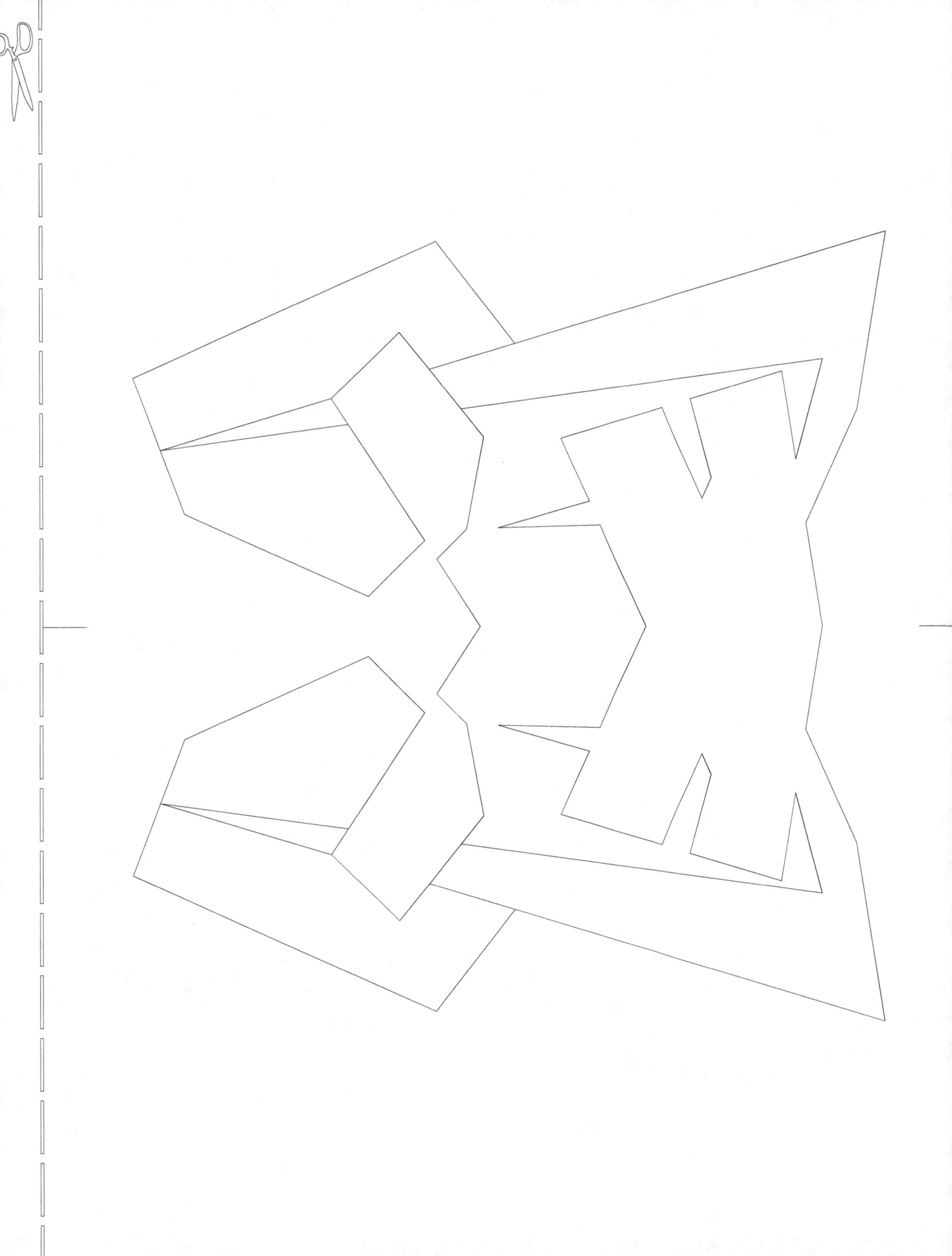

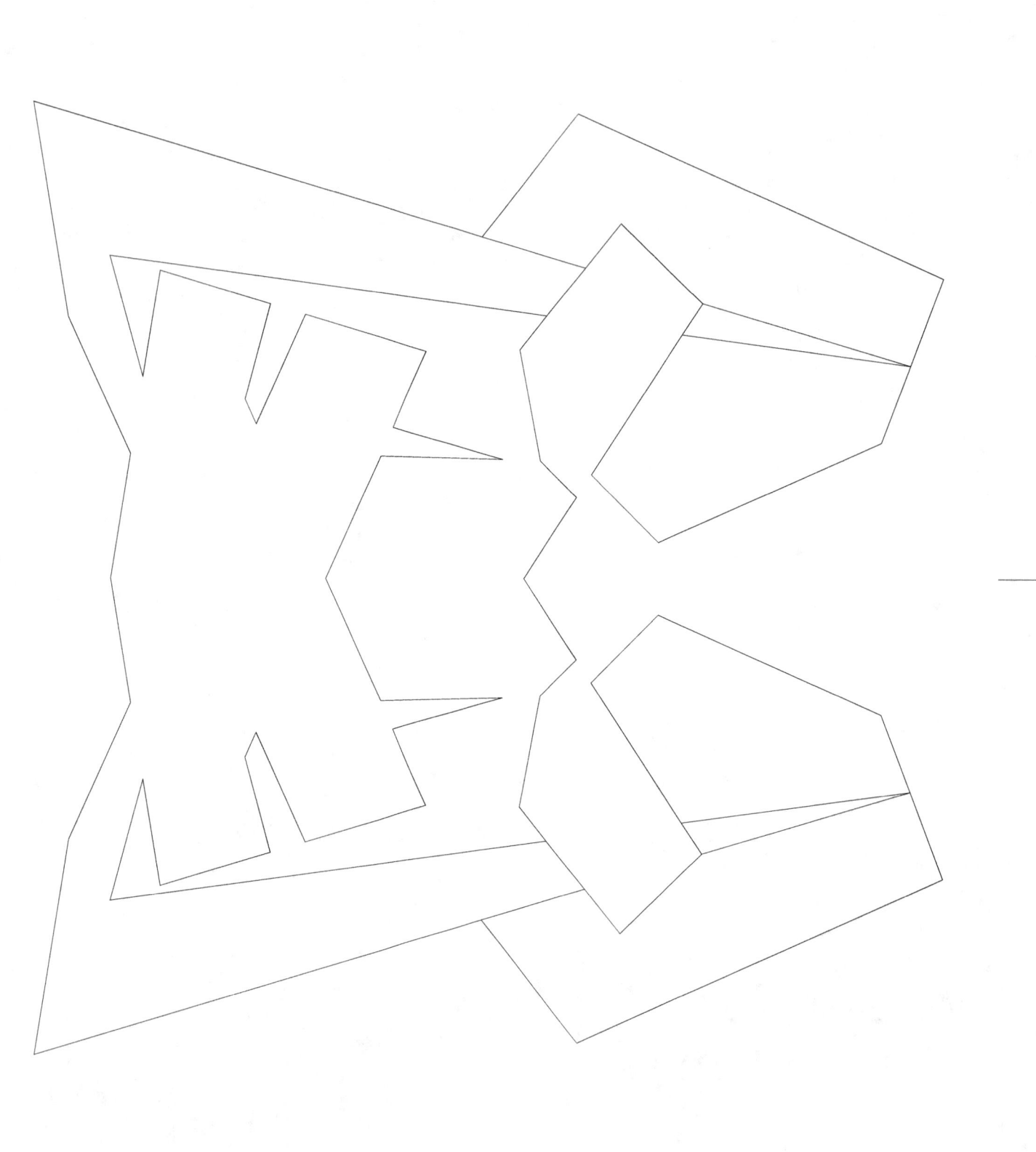

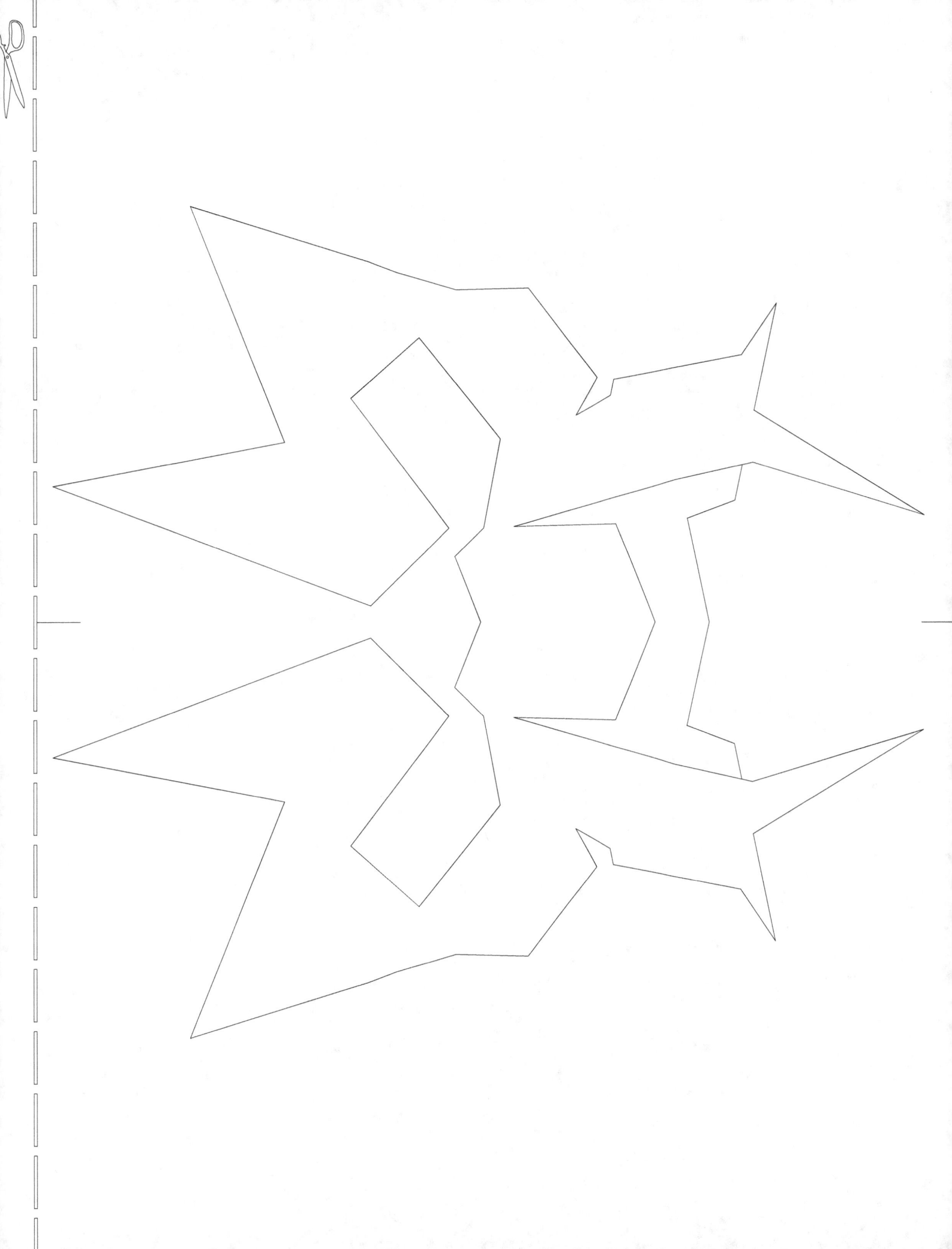

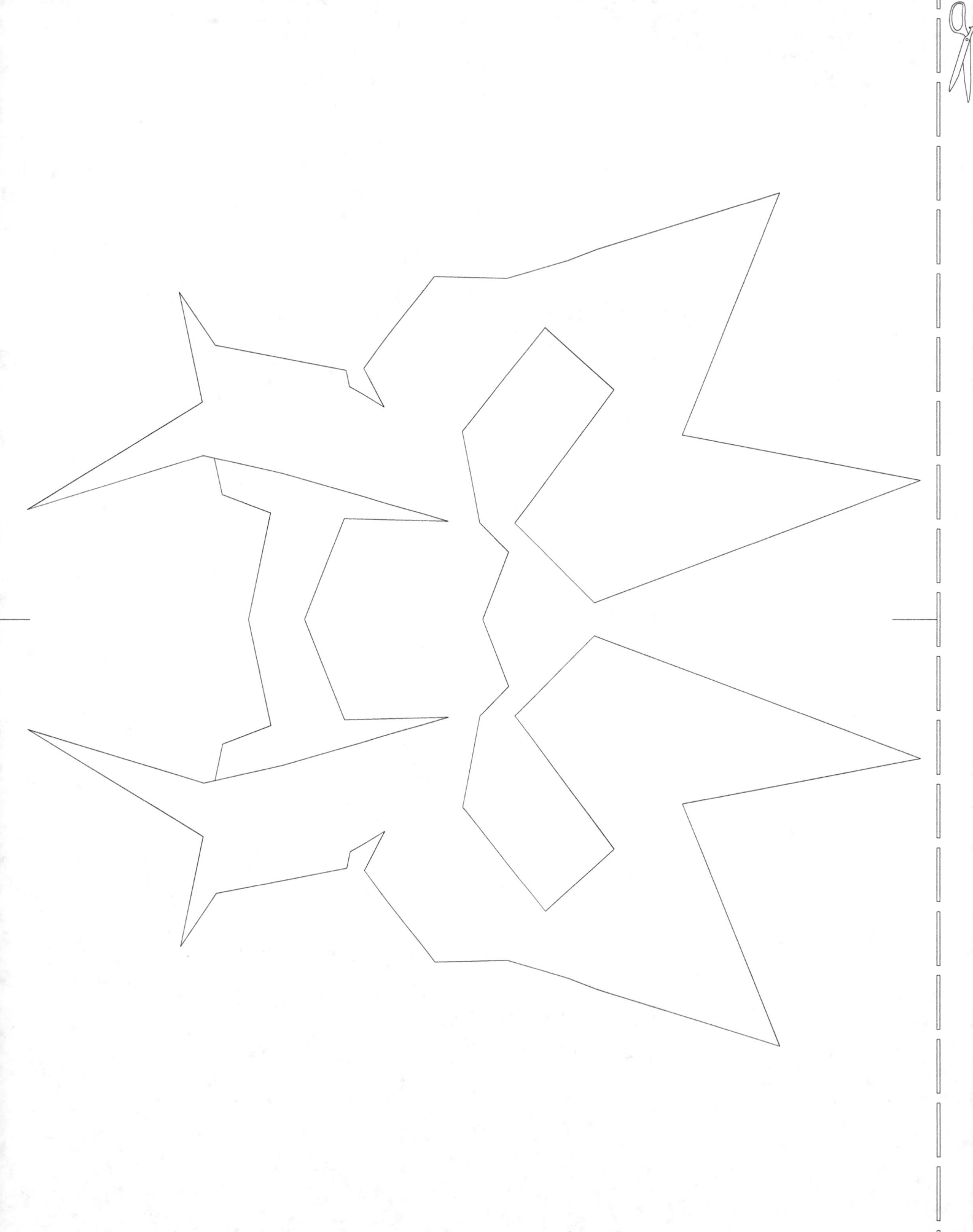

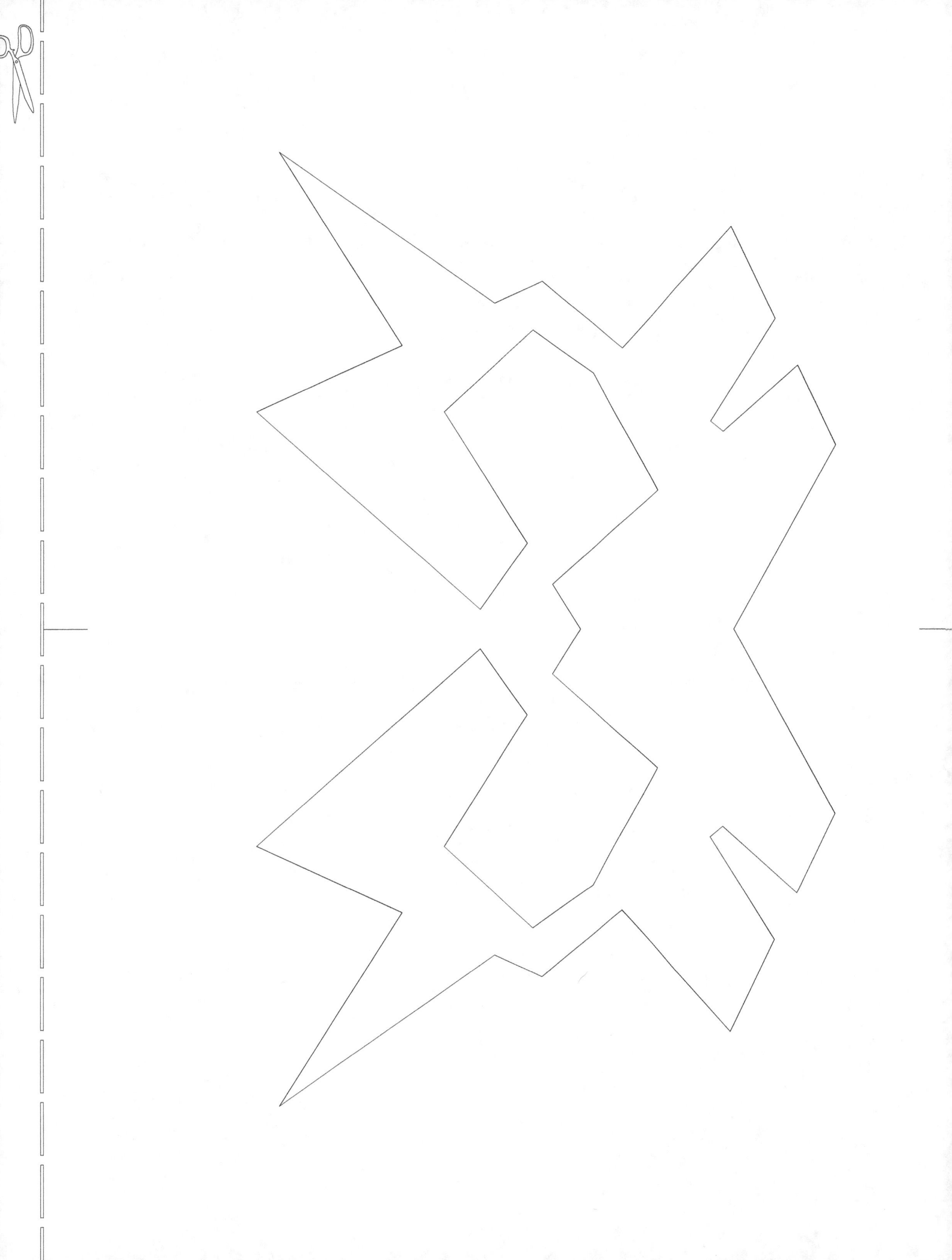

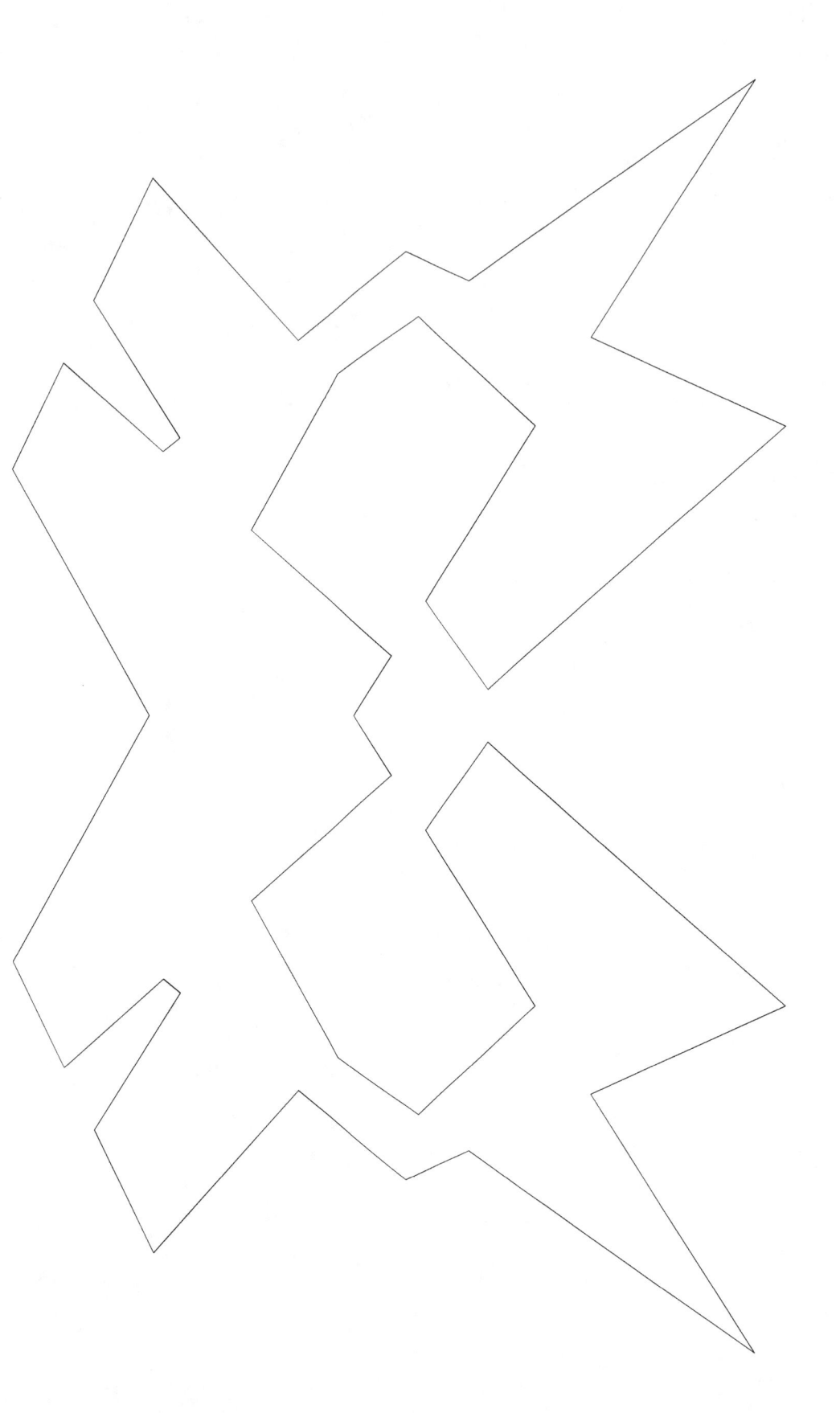

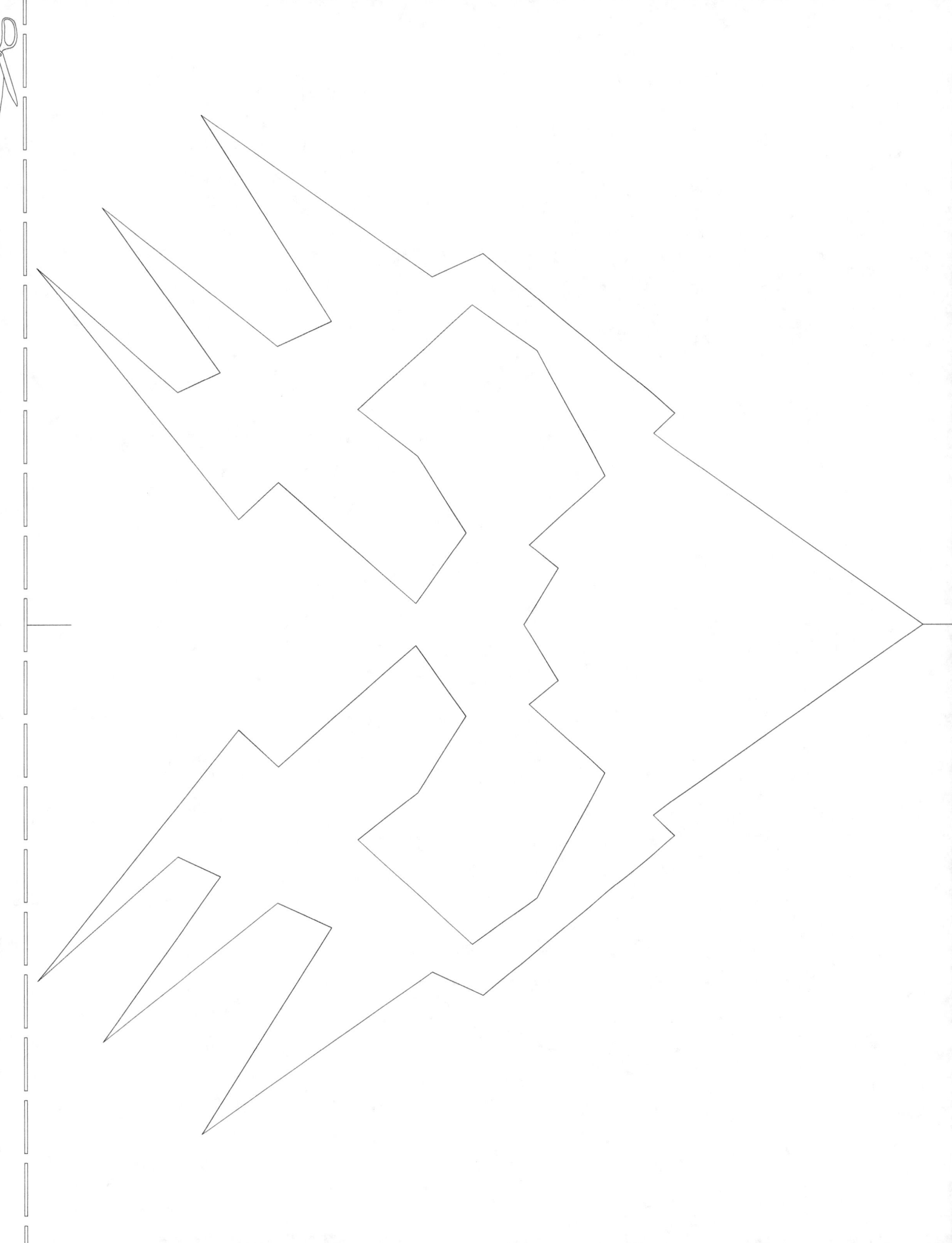

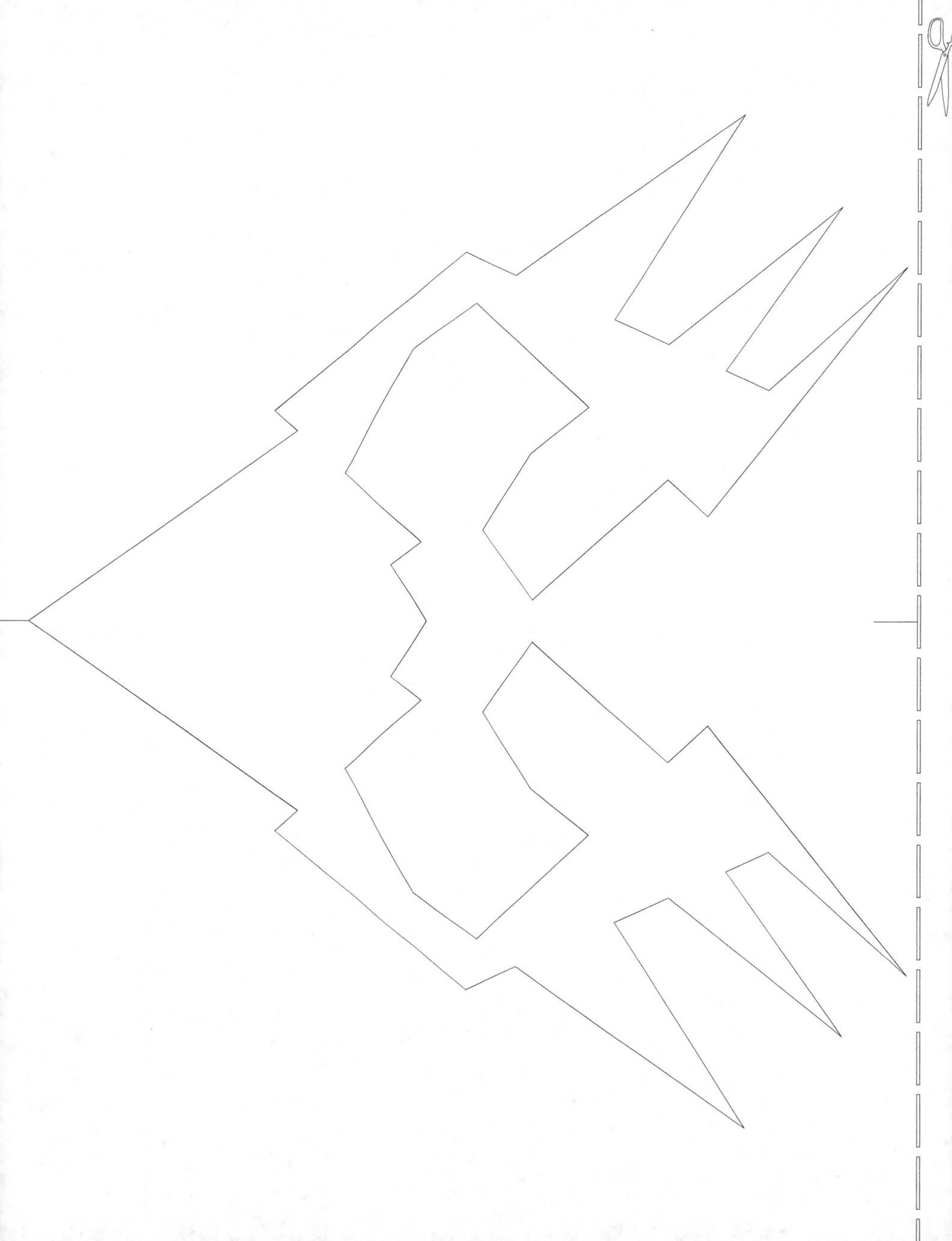

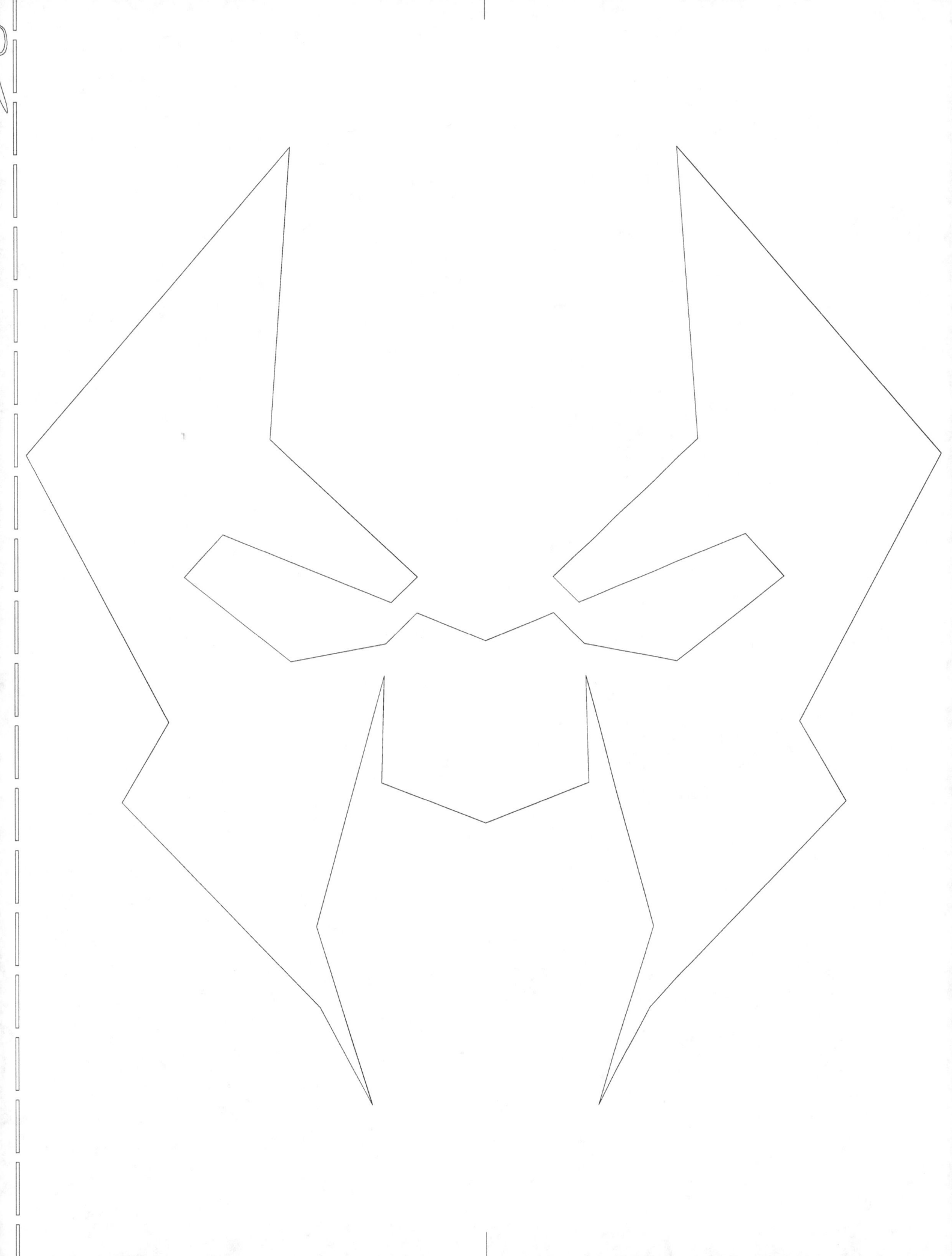

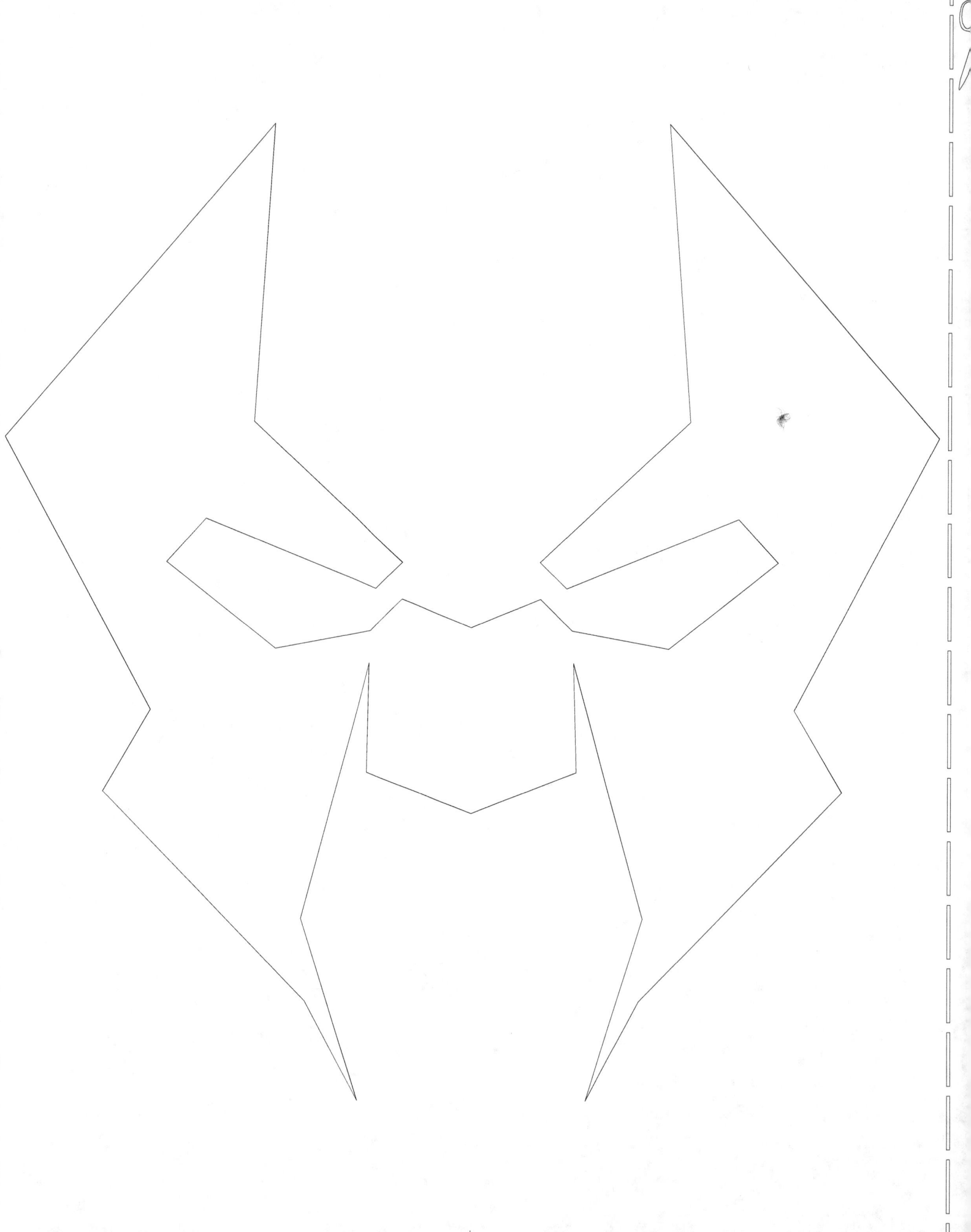

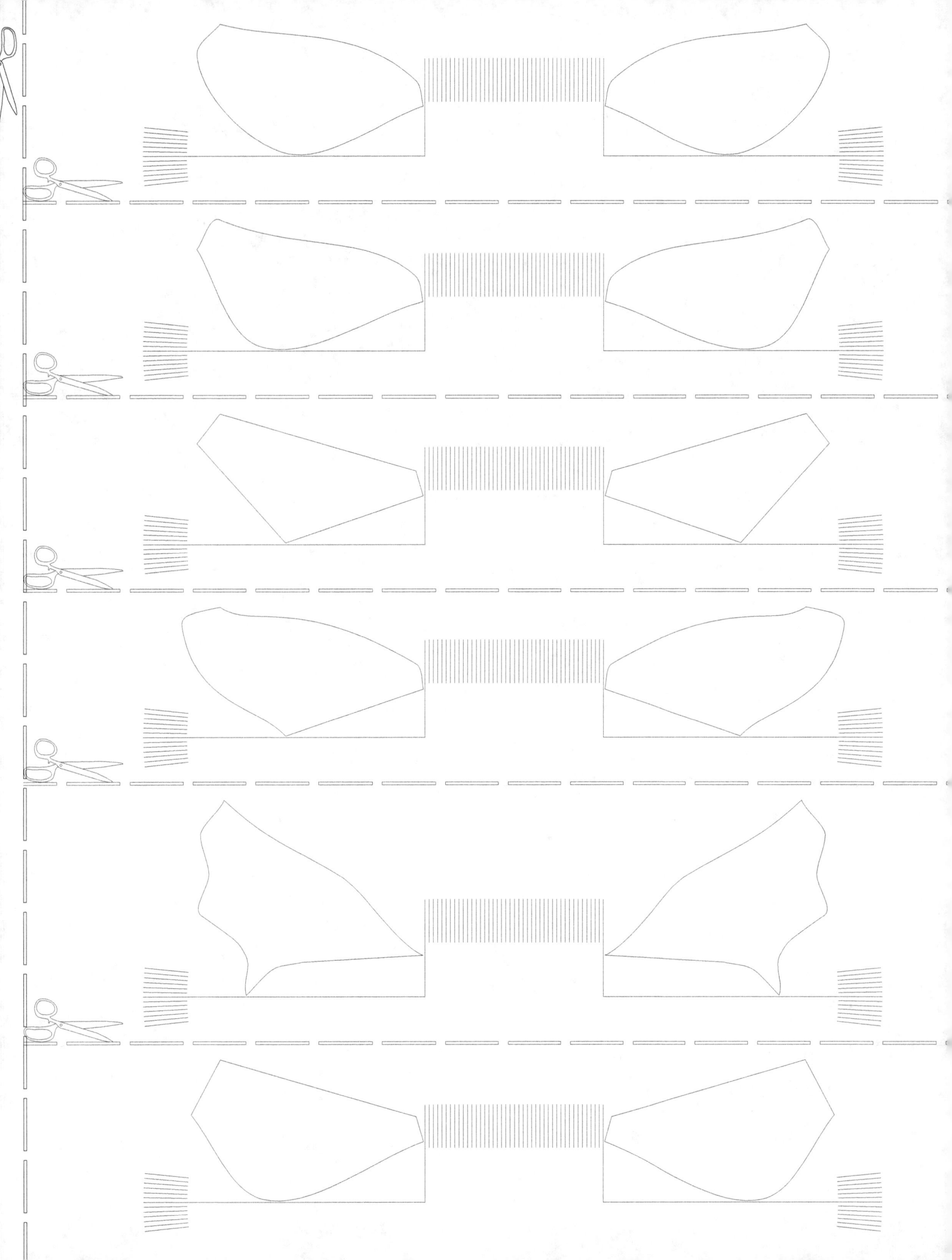

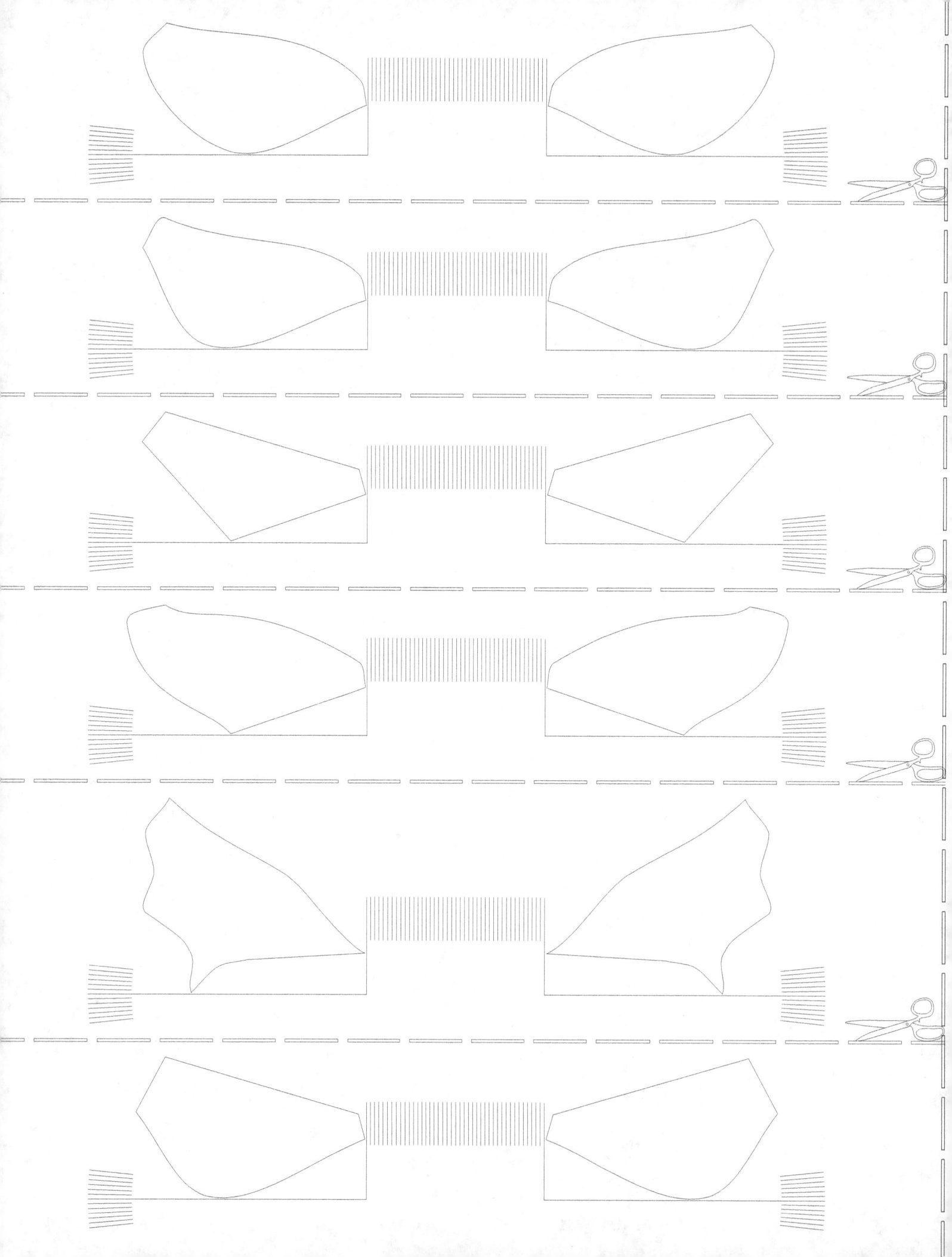

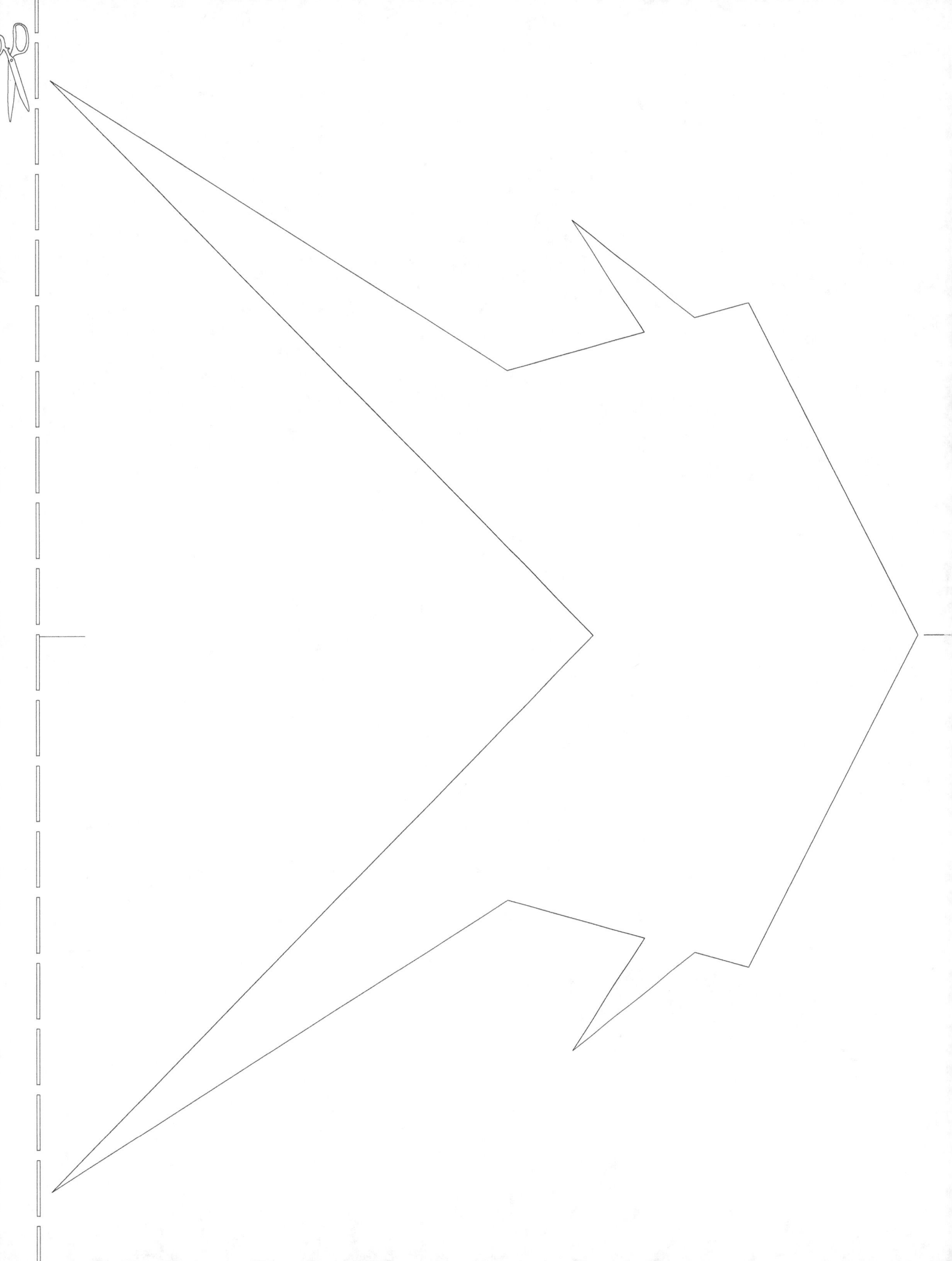

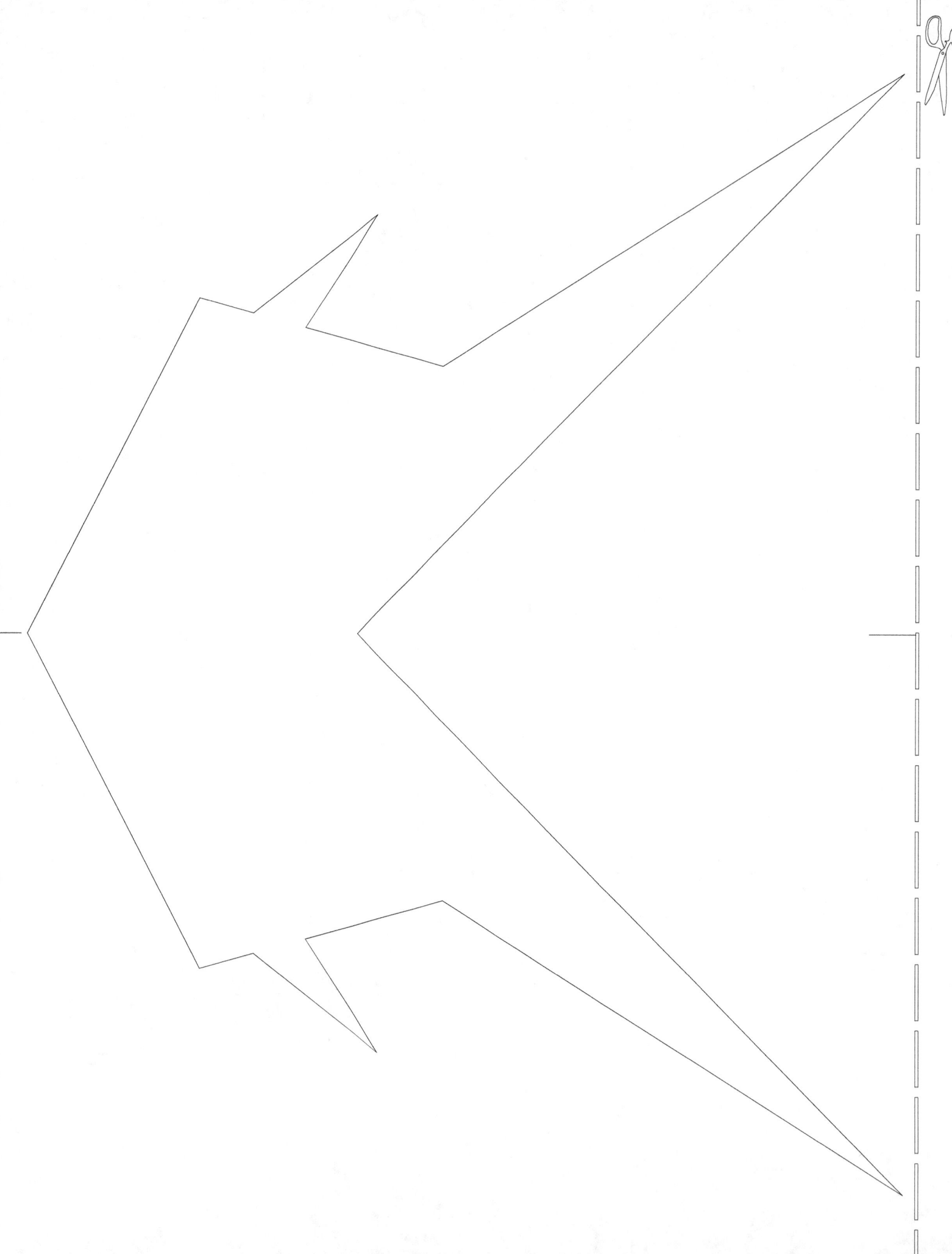

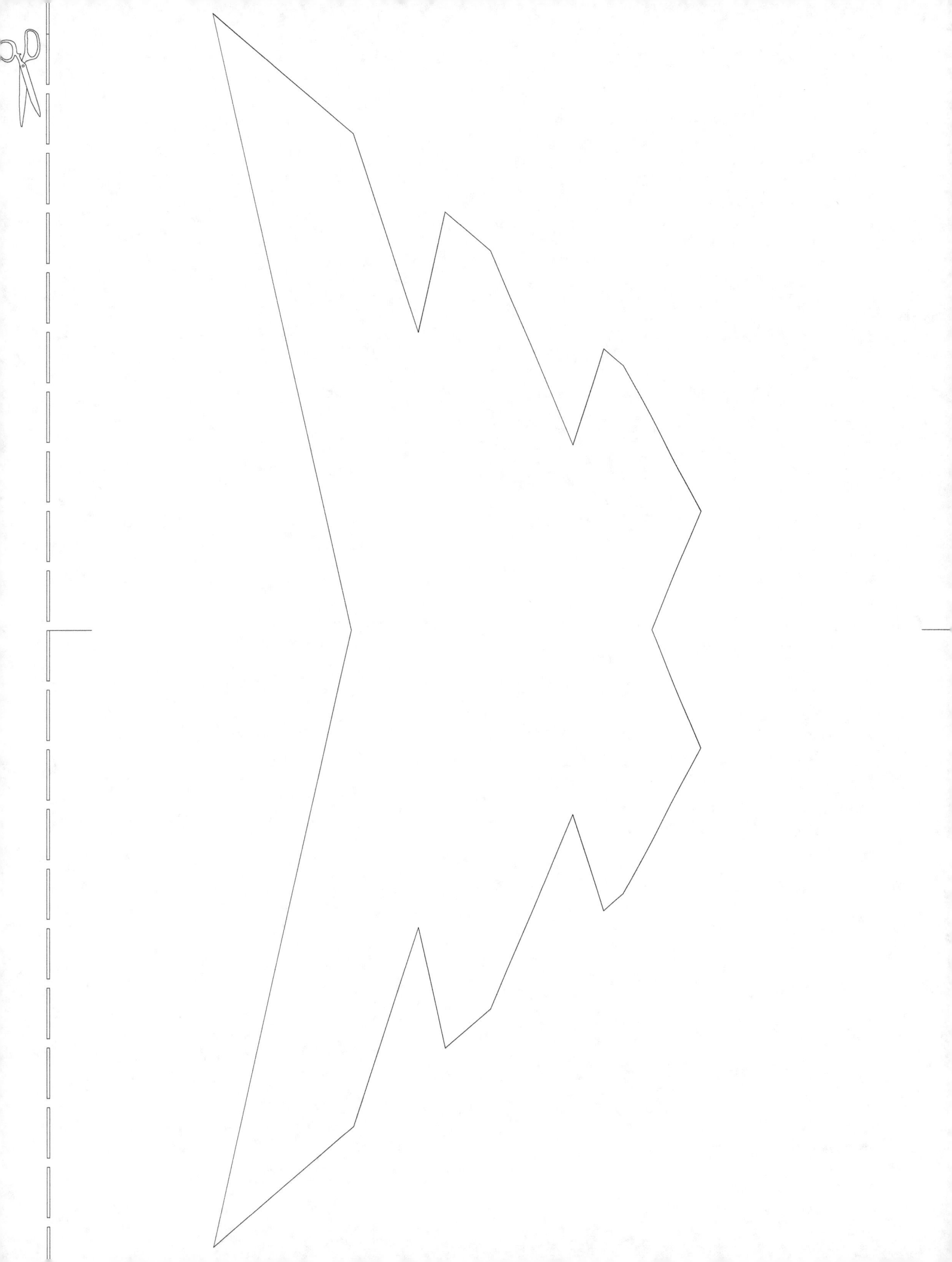

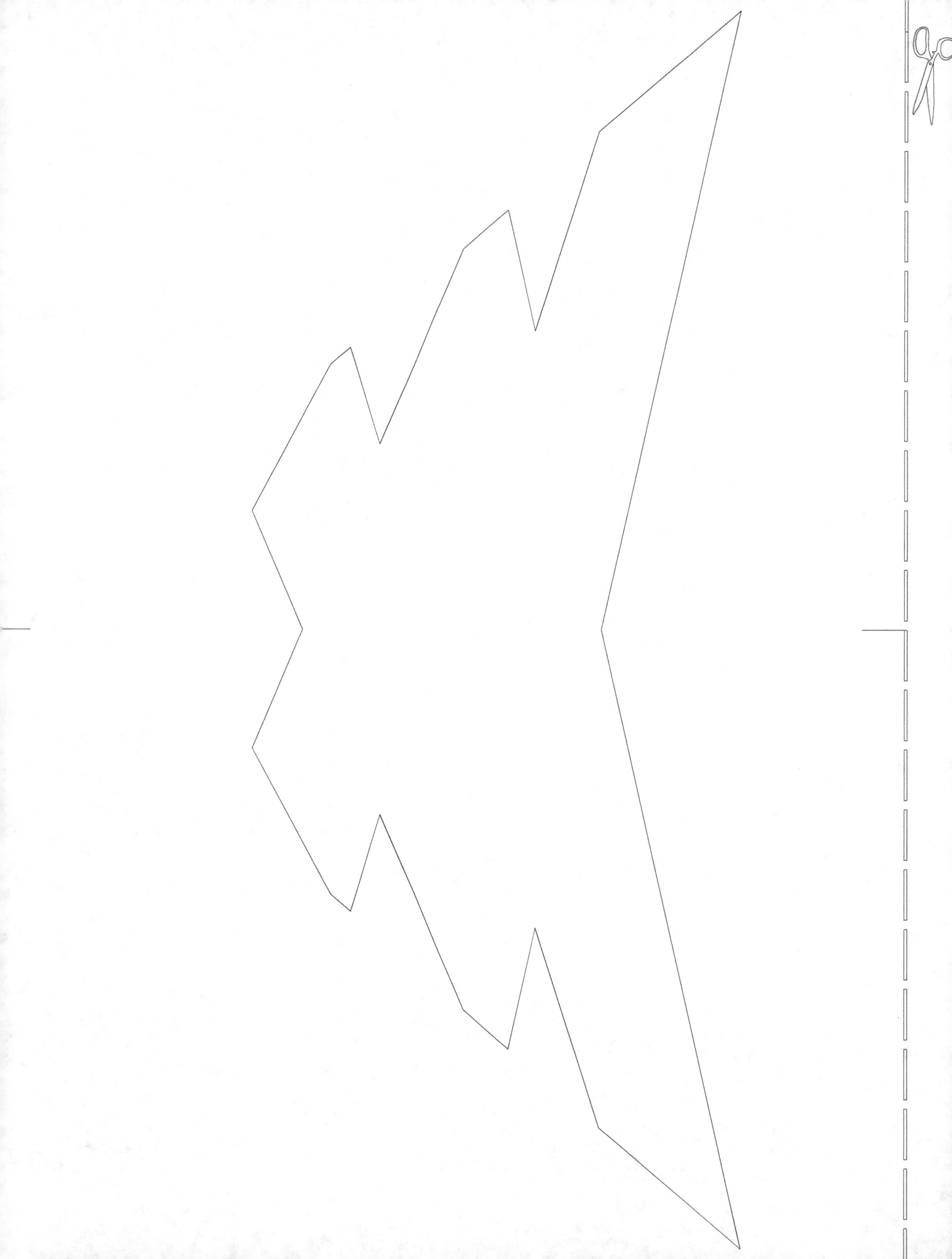

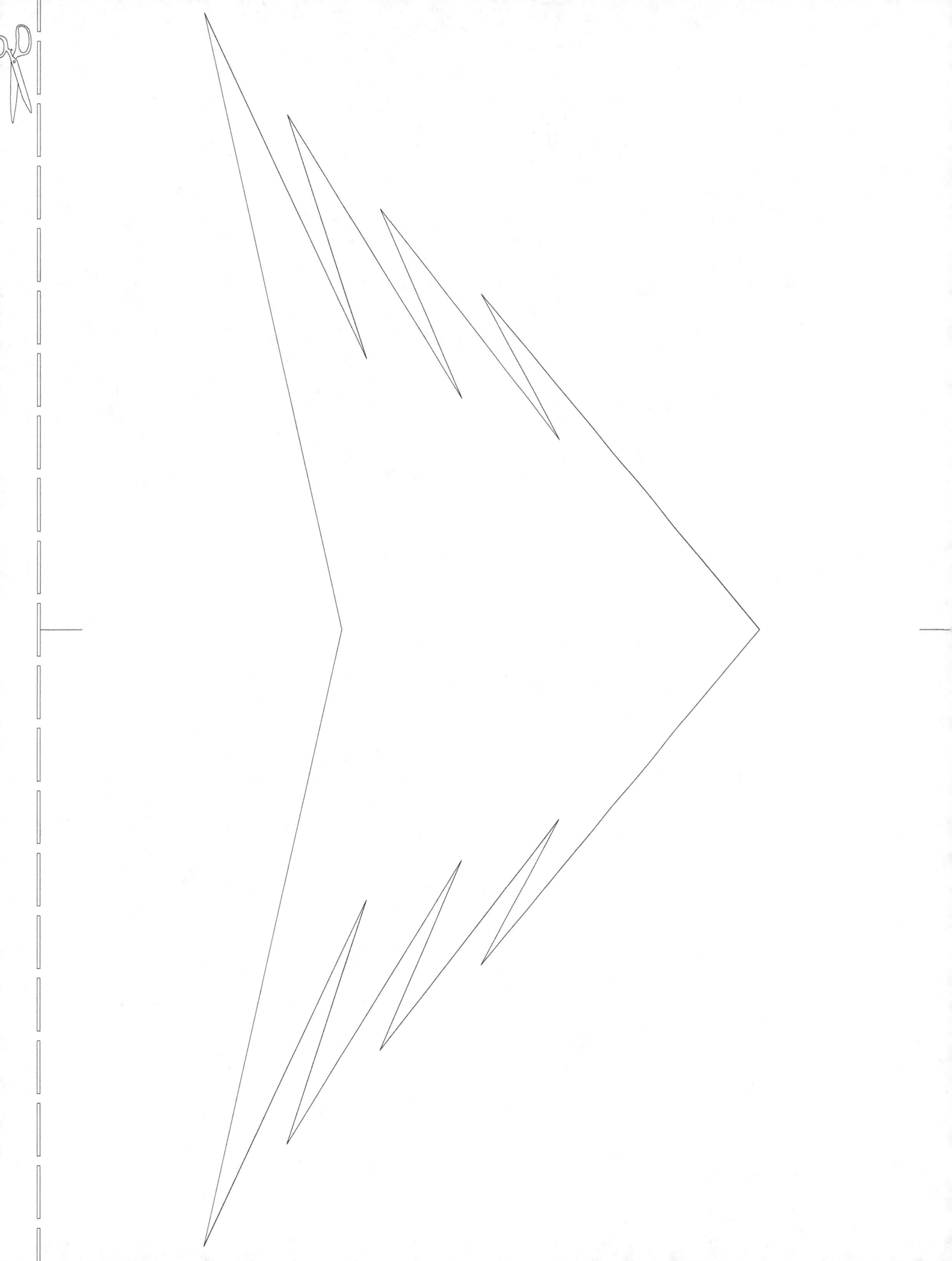

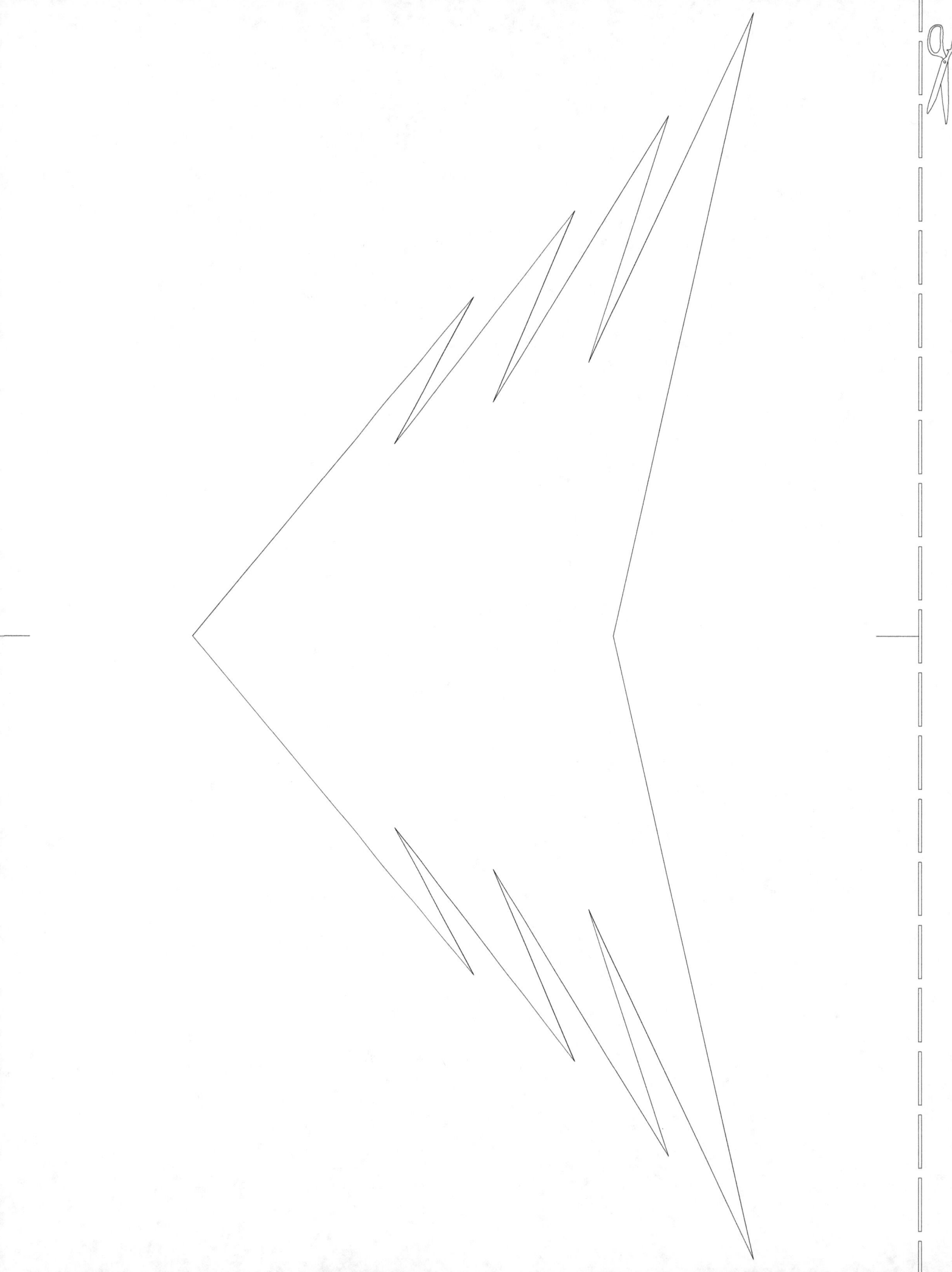

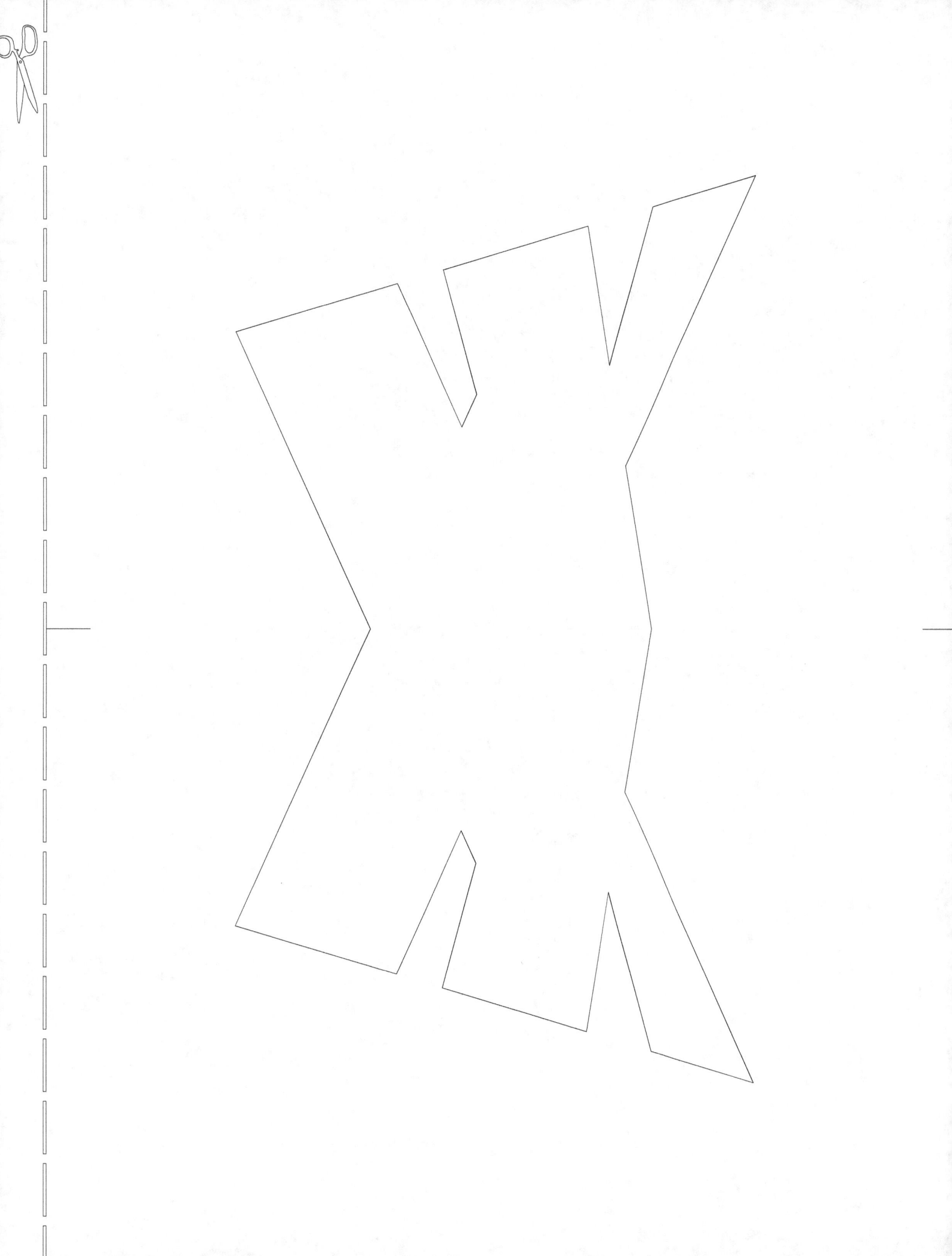

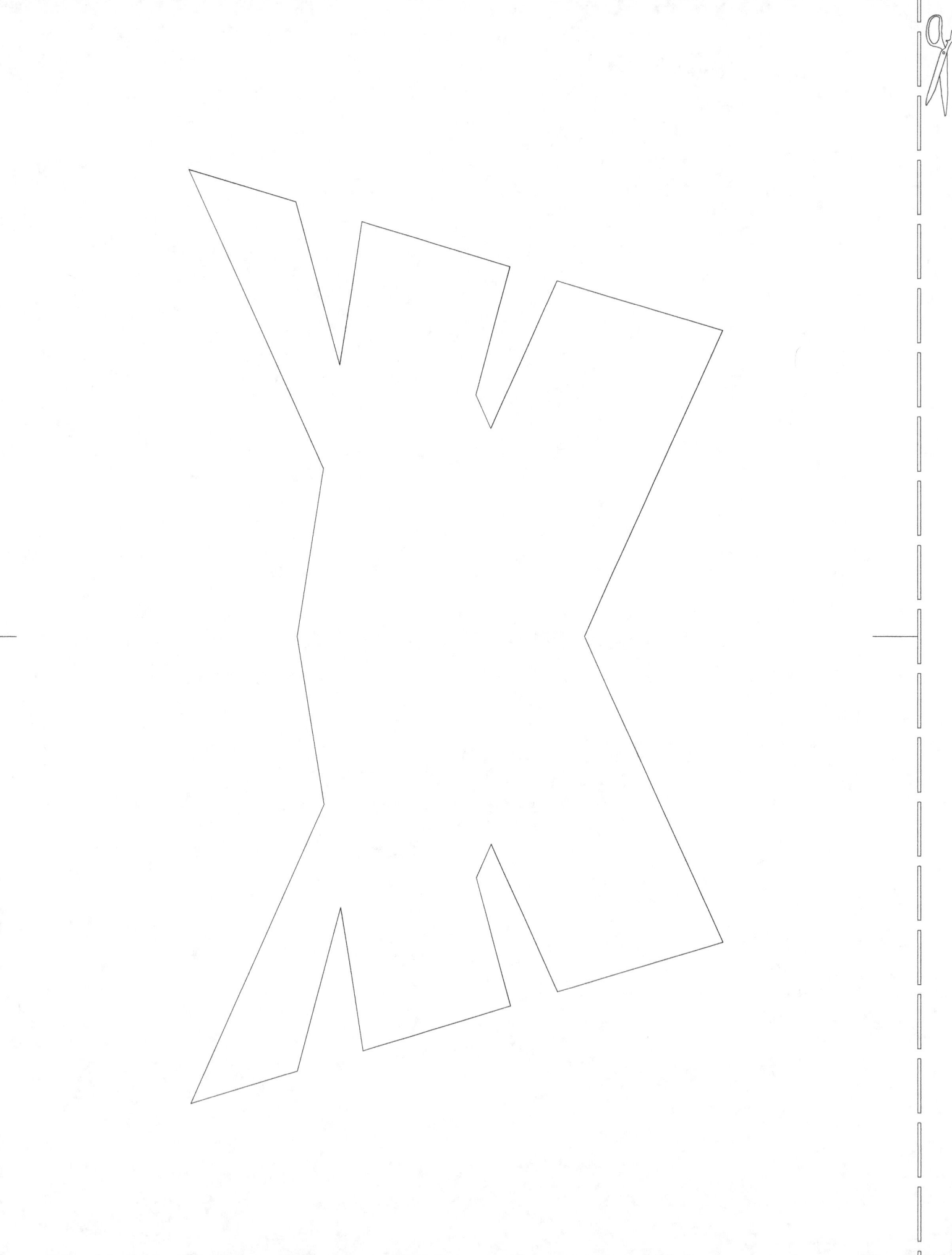

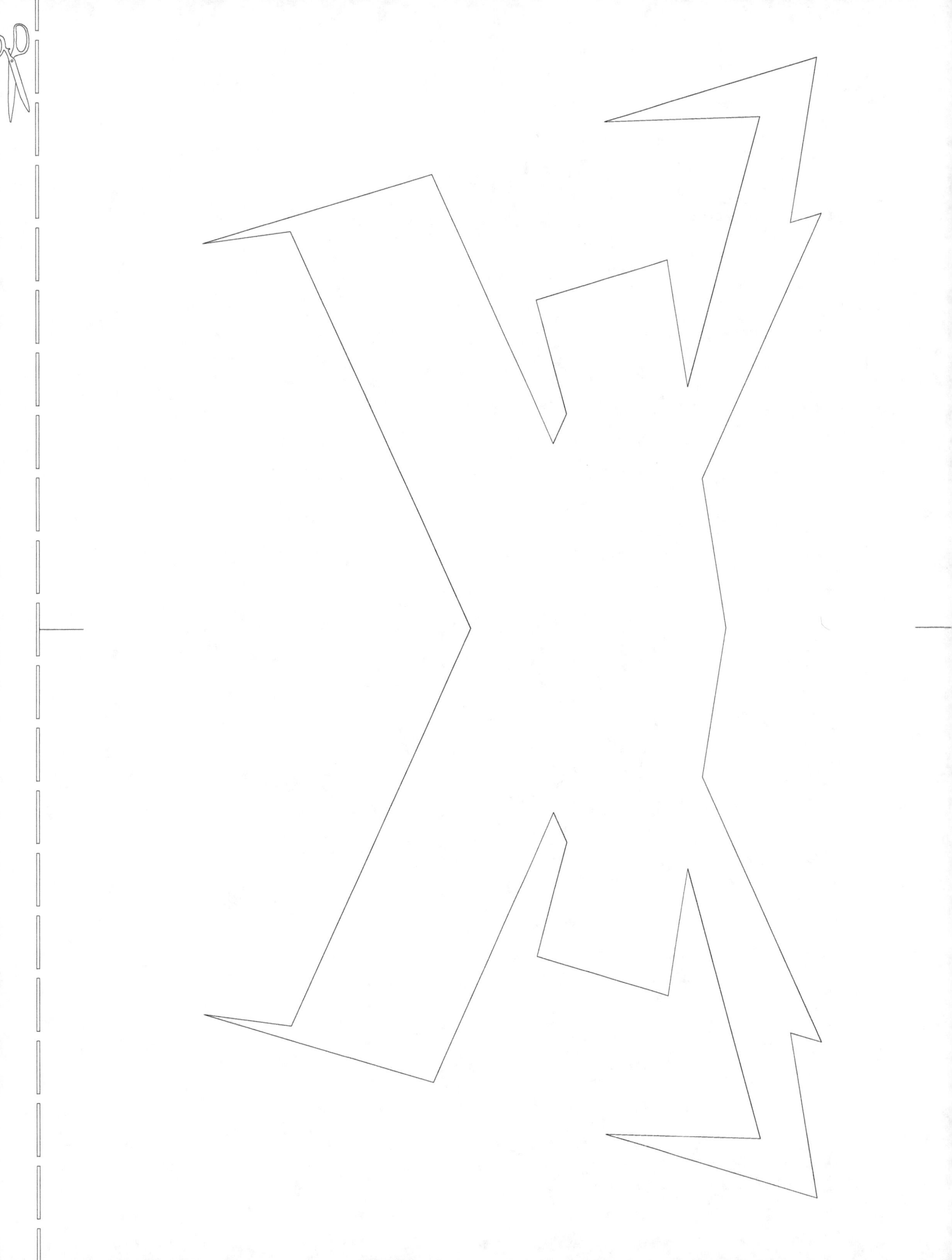

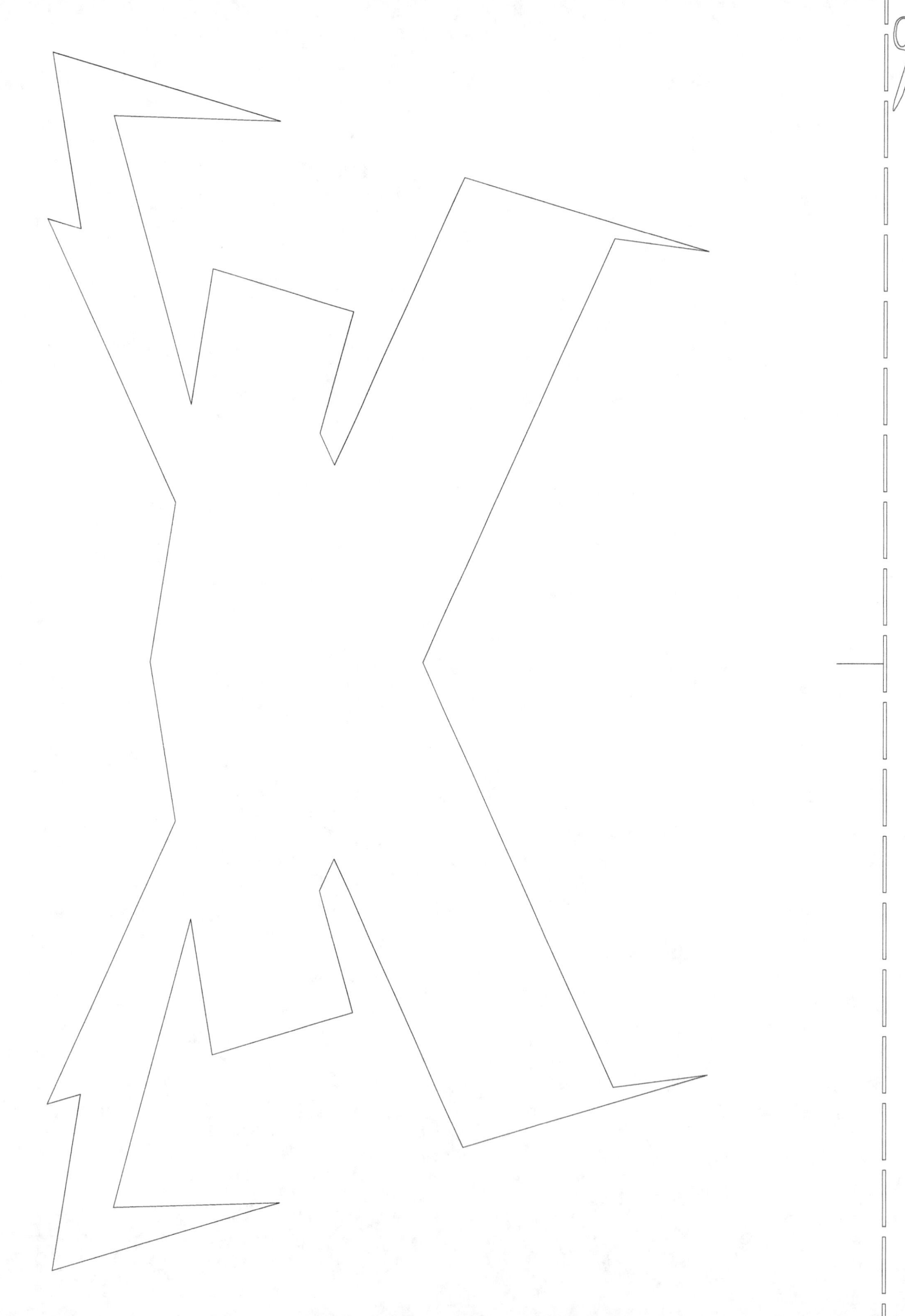

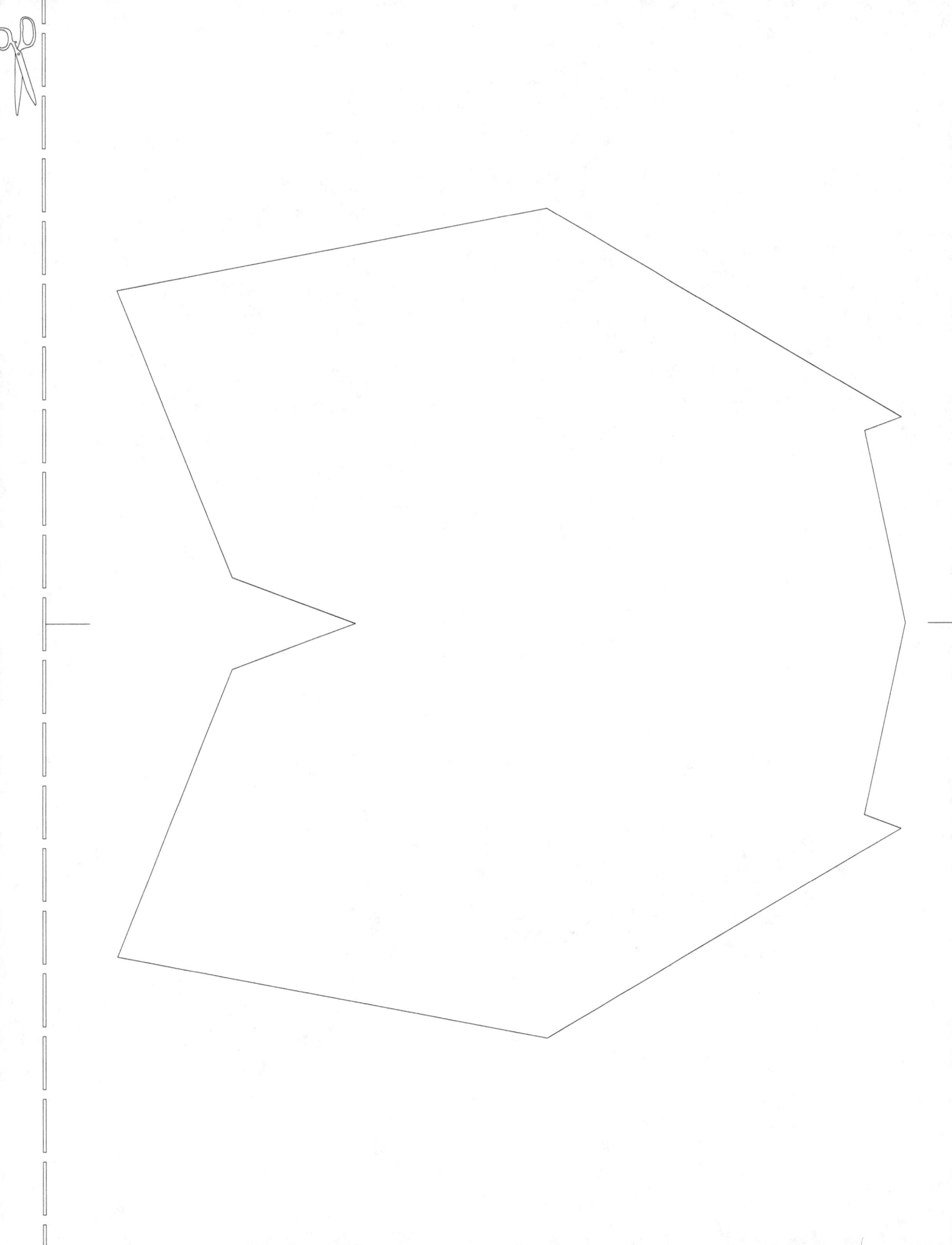

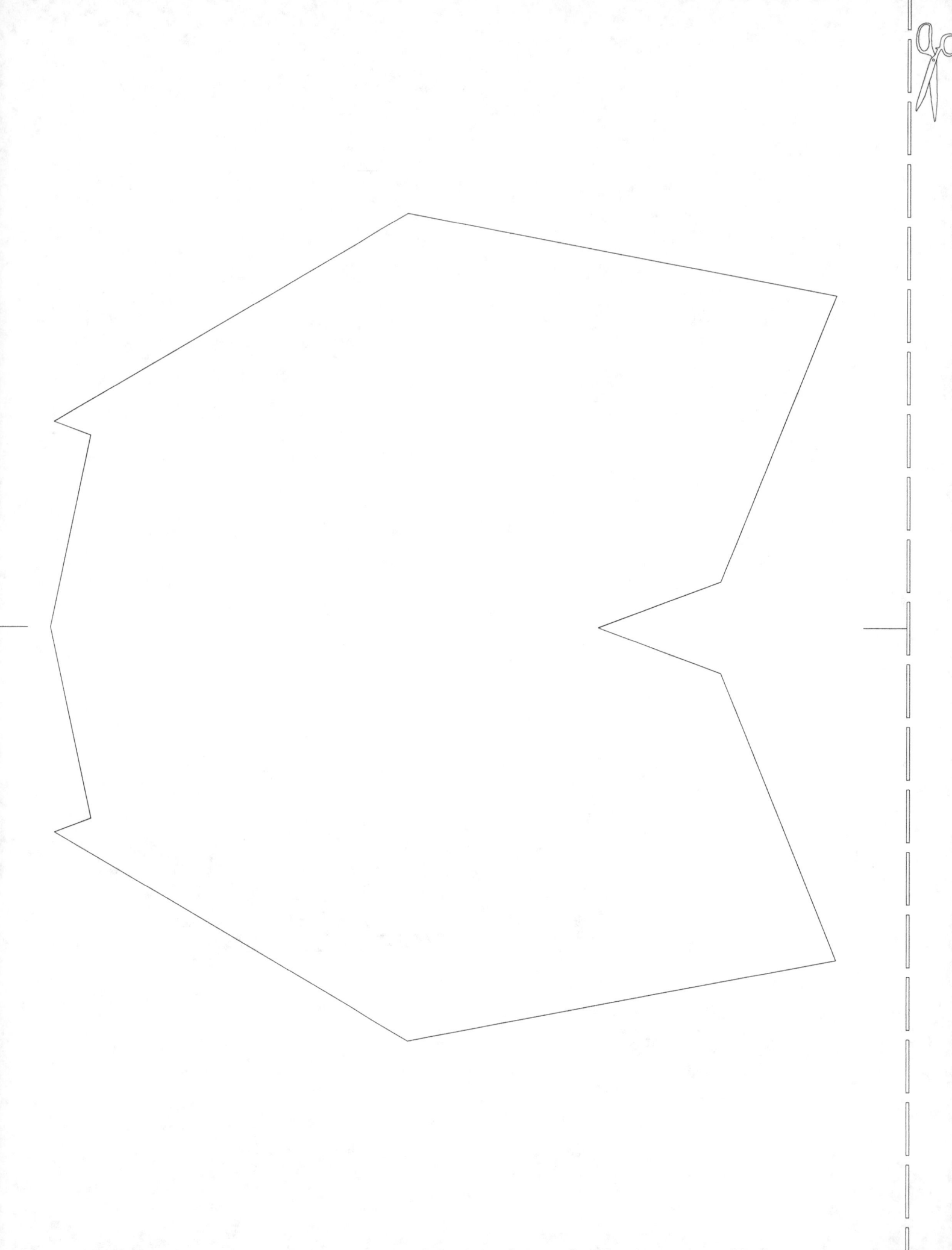

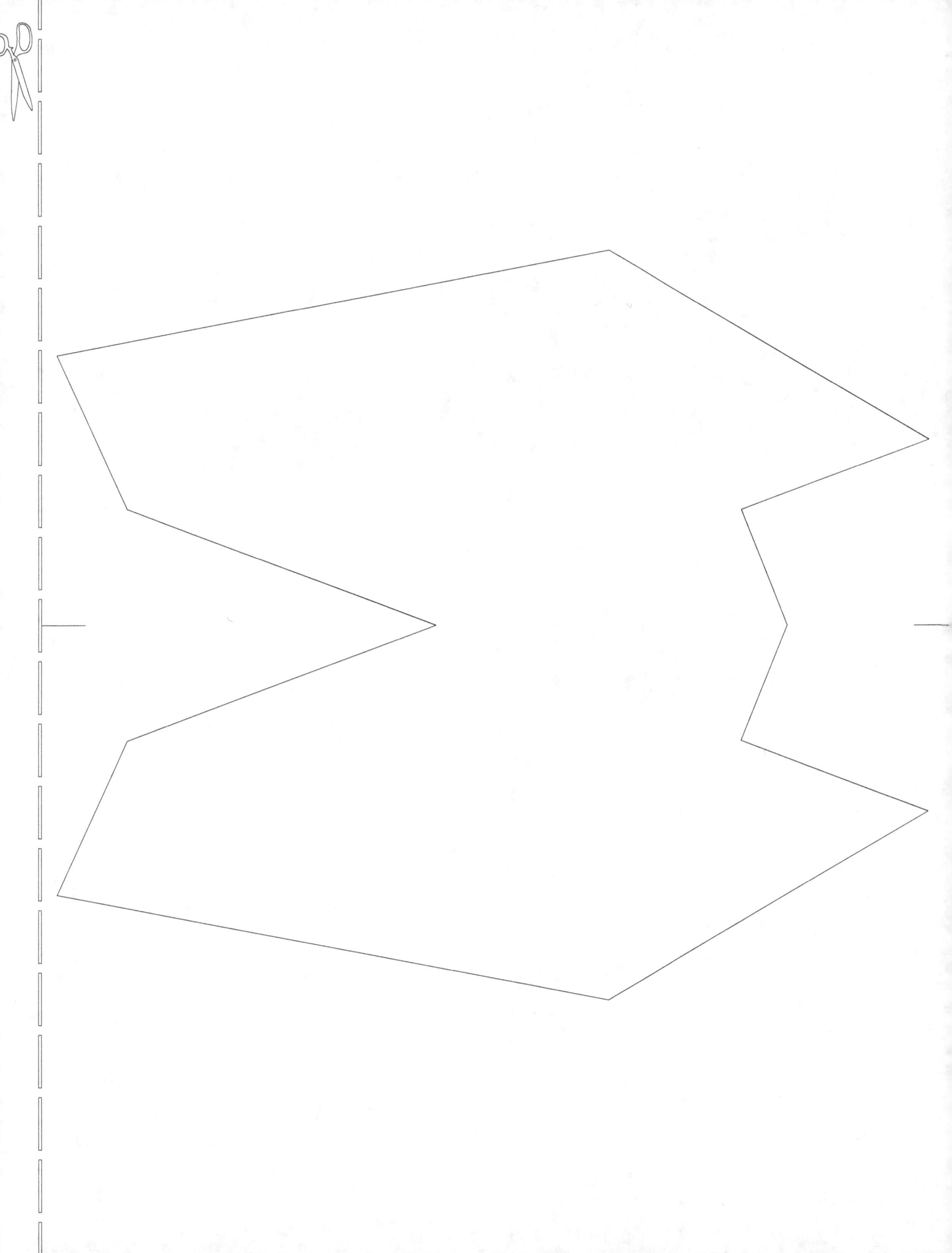

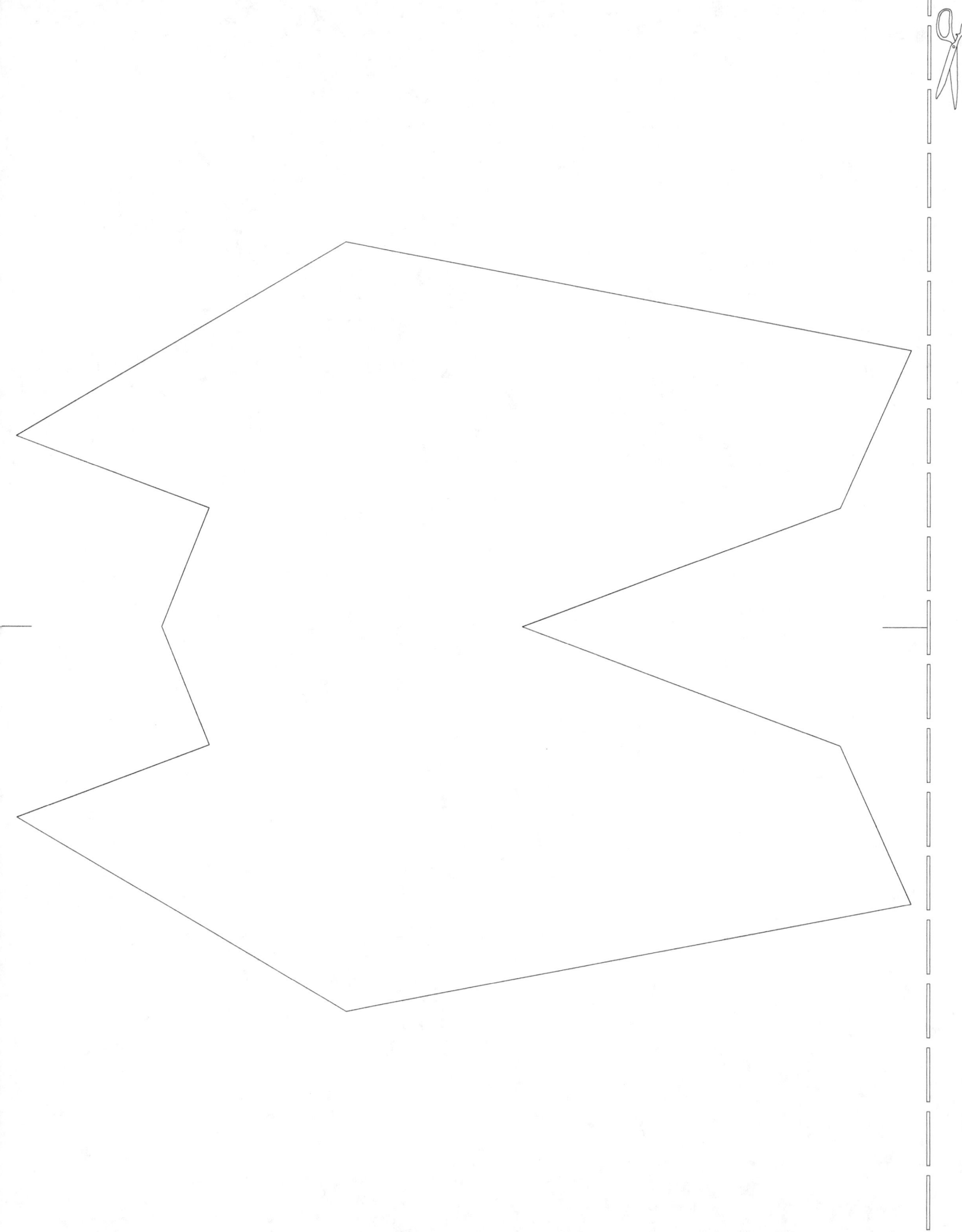

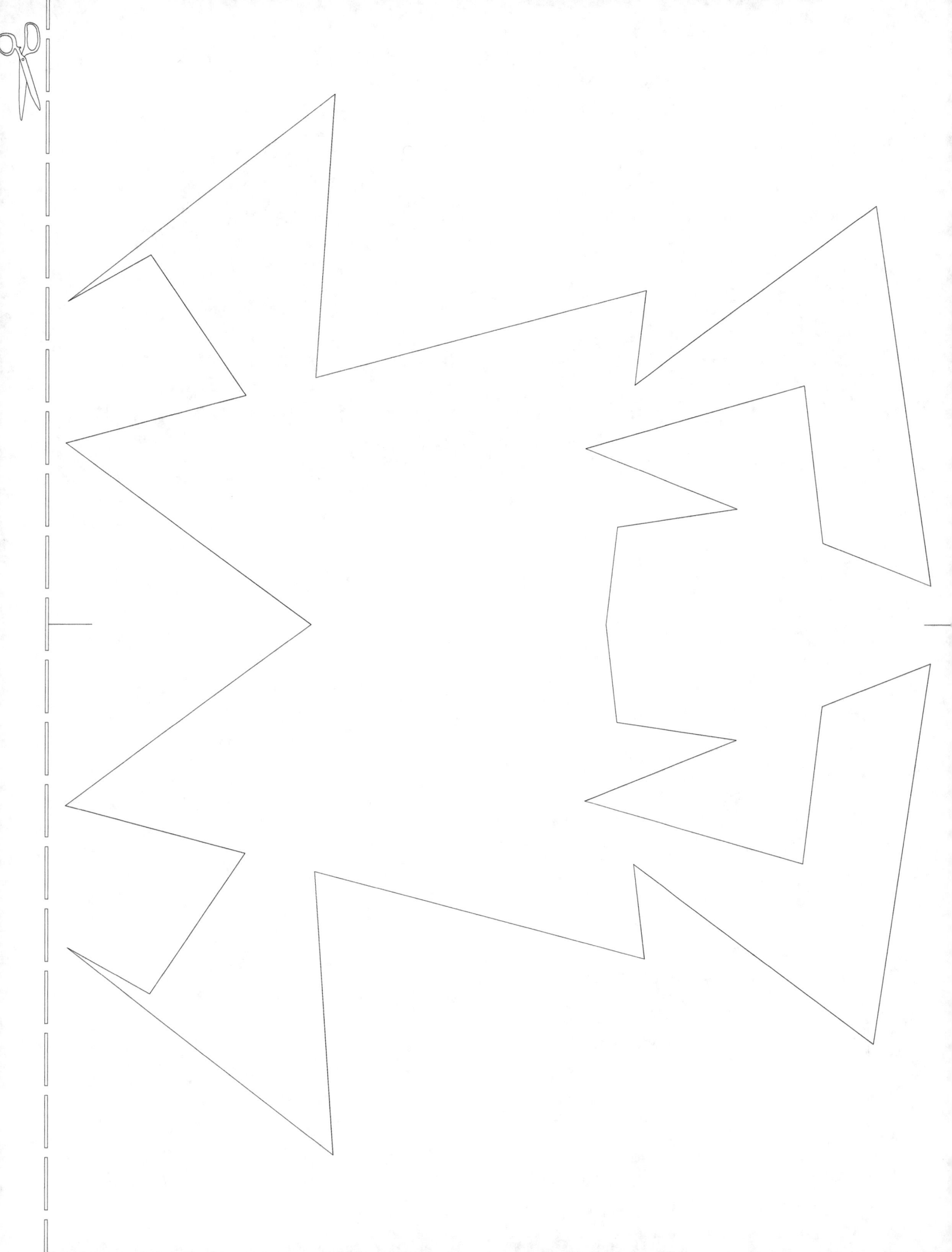

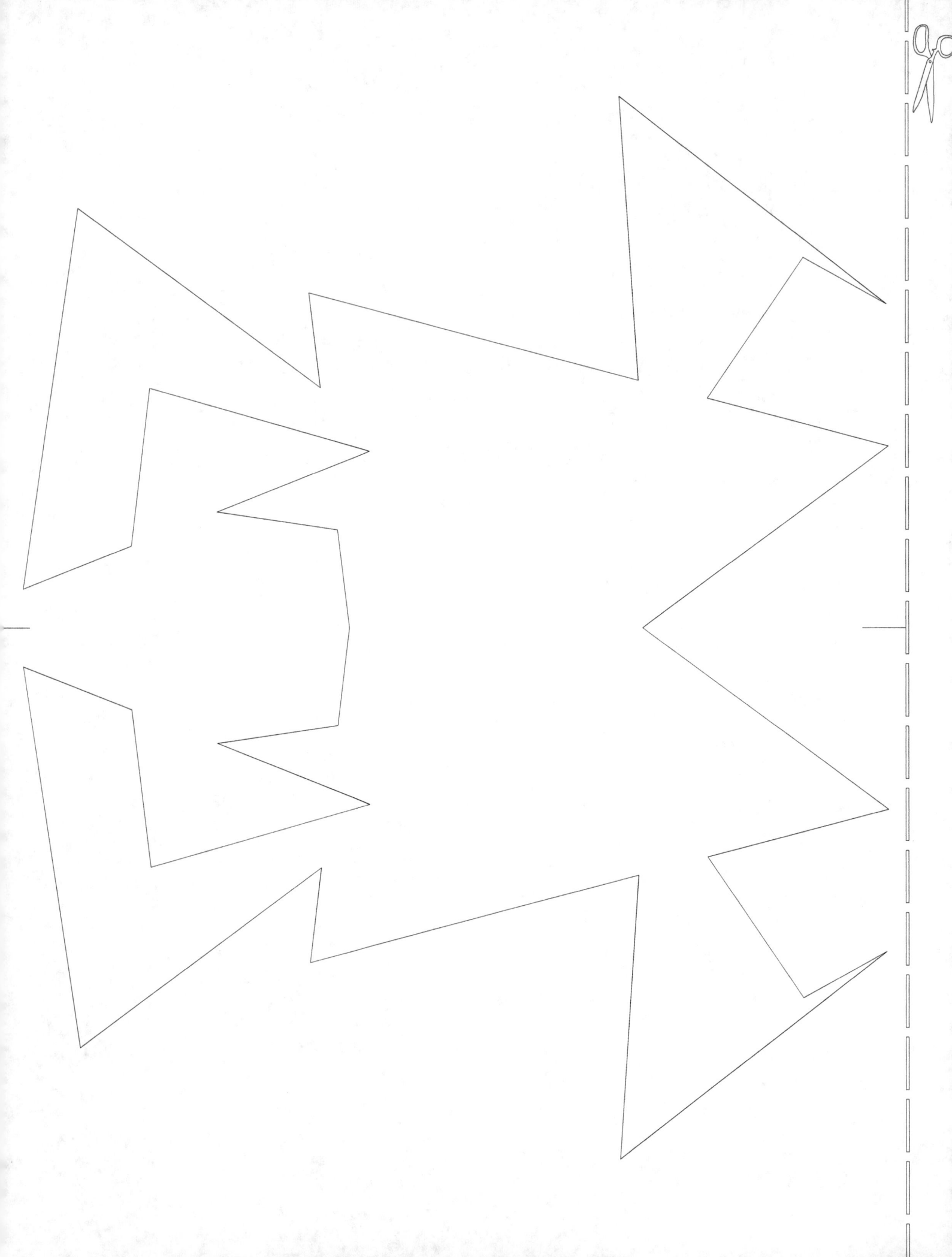

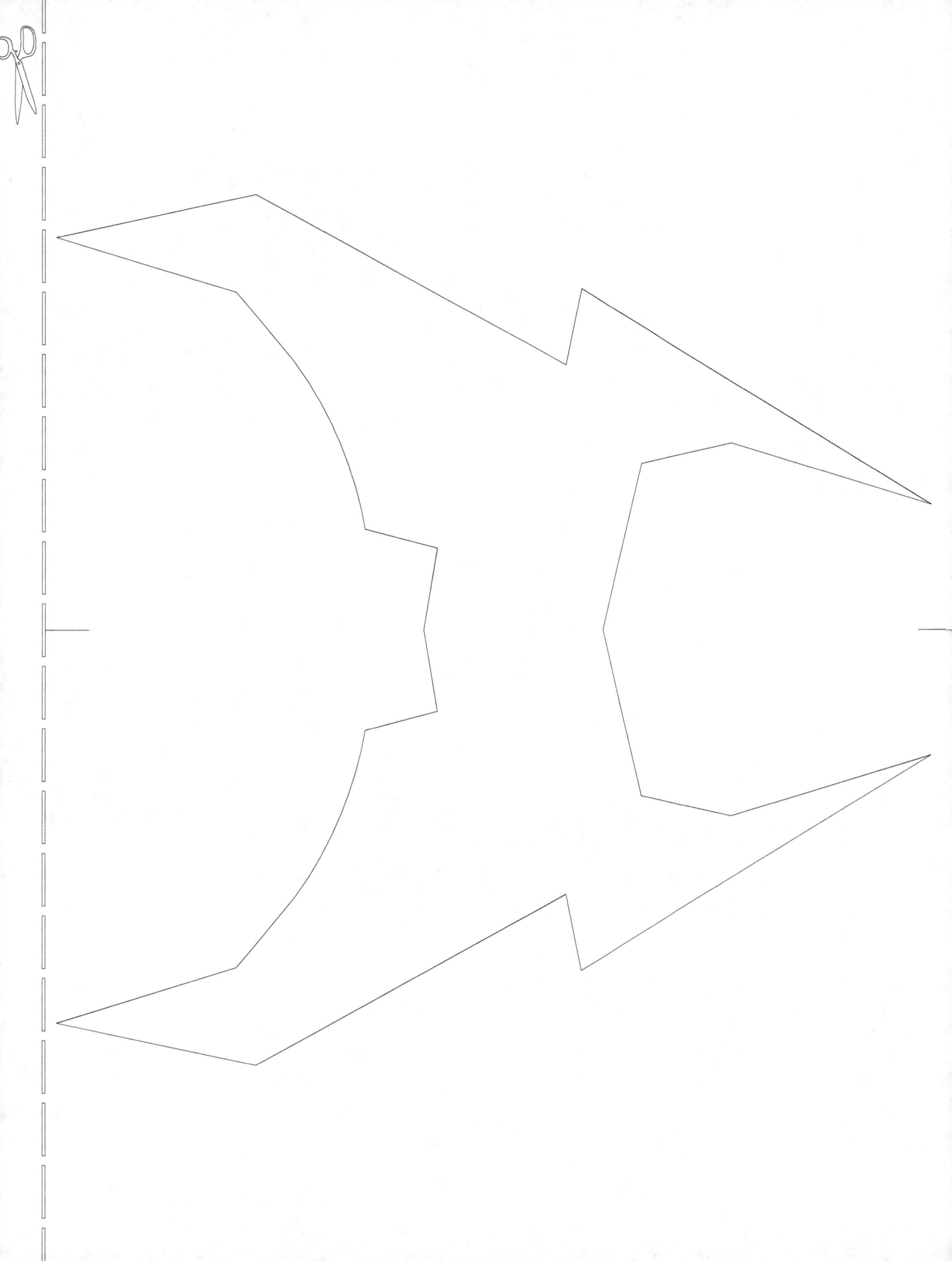

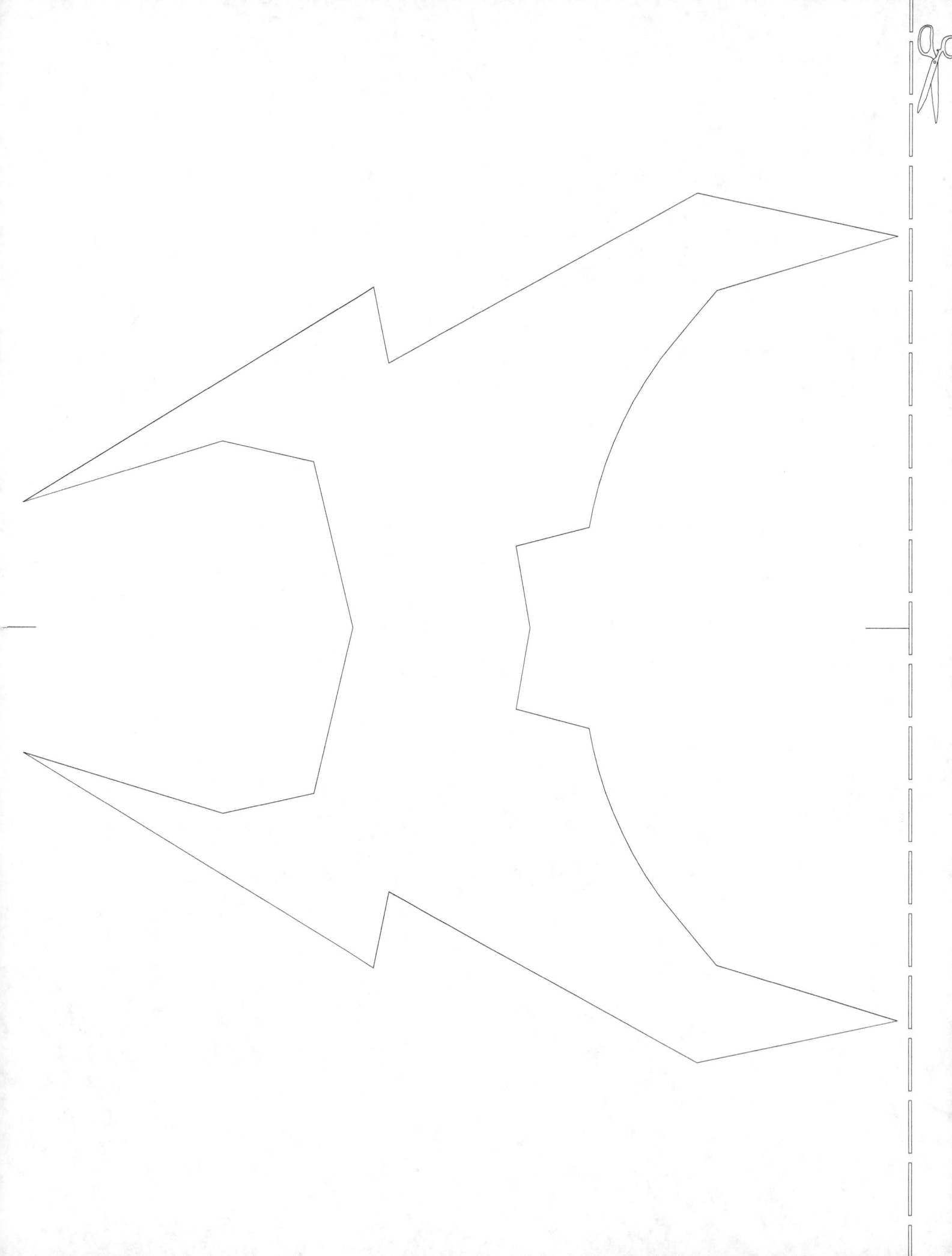

www.ingramcontent.com/pod-product-compliance
Lightning Source LLC
Chambersburg PA
CBHW081146170526
45158CB00009BA/2725